POLLS APART

KJ A REPORT
FROM THE KETTERING FOUNDATION

POLLS APART

John P. Robinson
Robert Meadow

SEVEN LOCKS PRESS
Cabin John, Md./Washington, D.C.

© 1982 by the Charles F. Kettering Foundation

Library of Congress Cataloging in Publication Data

Robinson, John P.
    Polls apart.

    Bibliography: p.
    Includes index.
    1. United States—Foreign relations—1945—Public opinion. 2.
Public opinion—United States.   3. Public opinion polls.   I. Meadow,
Robert G.   II. Charles F. Kettering Foundation.   III. Title.
E840.R55   327.73   82-853
ISBN 0-932020-12-7   AACR2

Book Design by Chuck Myers
Typography by Susan Kelly and Kaye Brubaker

Manufactured in the United States of America

SEVEN LOCKS PRESS, INC.
An affiliate of Calvin Kytle Associates
P.O. Box 72
Cabin John, Md. 20818

Let every man make known what kind of government would command his respect, and that will be one step toward obtaining it.

—HENRY DAVID THOREAU
"Civil Disobedience"

We have always had differences of opinion which have produced confusion in this country—especially in campaign years. But it is the kind of noise that, to the inner ear, is the sweet music of free institutions. It is the kind of noise that has produced the harmony of firm purpose whenever our people have been put to the test.

—ADLAI STEVENSON
Speech, 9 September 1952
San Francisco, California

Vox populi, vox humbug.
—WILLIAM TECUMSEH SHERMAN
Letter to his wife
2 June 1863

Foreword

DESPITE THE CONSTITUTIONAL TRUMP that makes the people sovereign in the American political system, our nation has been unable to arrive at a settled view of how government should respond to public opinion.

This ambivalence is understandable. There are many Americas. Our interests are diverse; we do not speak with one voice. To the elected official who tries to sort out these voices, a tractable public is an easy partner in shaping policy while a contrary public is, in Lippmann's phrase, a "bewildered herd." How we feel about public opinion depends on where we stand, where we think the public stands, and whose ox is being gored.

Whatever mixed emotions we may have about the role of public opinion, our recurring populist impulses will not let us ignore it. We are all fascinated by the public's tastes and inclinations. It, after all, is us—not a tidy singular but an unrepentant plurality.

Polls Apart originated in an unusual effort to improve two-way communication on foreign policy issues between the State Department and the American people. In 1976 and 1977, small groups of top Department officials traveled to foreign policy "town meetings" in ten cities. They listened closely to the views of representatives from a variety of constituencies. When they returned to Washington, they reported their findings and impressions to the secretary of state.

But were the opinions aired in the town meetings representative? Foreseeing this challenge, the organizers proposed taking local polls on the same foreign policy issues that were discussed in the meetings. This city-wide random sample, interviewed by telephone, would shed light on local elite opinion; by the same token, the town meeting would provide a perspective for interpreting the metropolitan poll. And both could be compared to the results of national polls.

The Kettering Foundation offered to commission the series of metropolitan polls and asked Dr. John Robinson to manage them. We were immediately attracted to this extraordinary example of give-and-take between citizens and federal officials. We also saw it as an opportunity to encourage opinion research specialists with a critical turn of mind to help us, and others, probe what is wrong with polling on policy issues and what ought to be done about it.

Polls Apart examines these questions. It is about the conceptual and methodological problems of investigating and characterizing opinions on foreign policy issues, and the perceptions and values that lie behind them. In their provocative study, Robinson and coauthor Robert Meadow go beyond standard criticisms of error in question construction, sampling, interviewing, and data analysis. They argue that opinion research would be a more subtle and powerful tool for policy makers if it enabled them to understand public opinion as a complex pattern of demographic, psychological, and ideological factors. This will require, they say, a "representative ethnography."

As I look back on the foreign policy town meetings and other public opinion and policy education ventures, it becomes increasingly clear to me that the question of public influence on the policy process is plagued by flawed assumptions, partial or distorted images of social reality, and language that fails to do reality justice. Both liberal and conservative preconceptions can be faulted.

We need ideas, imagery, and language that catch the

complexity, the concurrence and dissonance of feelings and judgments on matters of public weight. The insight needed by opinion leaders and policy makers—needed, indeed, by everyone who is attentive to issues—requires a change of intent as well as a change of practice. Newspapers and their readers, television and its viewers will have to foreswear polls as gossip. They must start looking at polling as one of several interdependent methods for exploring public opinion.

The goal of this larger research should be to unfold the meaning of disparate opinions for policy choices and trade-offs. As Clifford Geertz suggests, the interpretation of social facts, including opinions, requires "systematic unpackings" of the symbolic worlds in which different people live.

The most revealing analysis of public sentiment, and its policy implications, begins by exploring the values and interests of the American people, "that tumultuous conglomeration of humanity." It asks how compatibilities and conflicts among groups in our society energize the political climate in which official ends and means are chosen. This is the promise of representative ethnography's approach.

An ethnographic strategy calls for the kind of methodological layering, or multiplicity of perspectives, in public opinion analysis that is found in anthropological field studies. These studies combine qualitative and quantitative methods to examine the roots and texture of a society's beliefs and values.

The ethnographic approach offers those who frame policy an interpretation of public opinion that, in Lincoln Bloomfield's words, will clarify our "definitions of the kind of nation we are and the kind of role we should play in the world—precisely that on which the people are, under our system, the *only* experts."

Policies that determine our nation's future, and invade

the destinies of other peoples, take their substance from the interplay between popular definitions, elite biases, and evangelical claims. In the last analysis, we are all at the mercy of the rifts and clashes among them.

In *Polls Apart*, Robinson and Meadow do not propose to do away with polling but to improve it by making opinion research both more precise and more perceptive. They still have faith that richer, more accurate information about public opinion will have, however indirectly and modestly, a favorable effect on the public policy of the American democracy, including its foreign policy. Their cautious optimism in the teeth of their own evidence is engaging. Pessimism would surely be defensible.

Phillips Ruopp
Vice President, Social Sciences
Charles F. Kettering Foundation

Preface

IN 1975, the Department of State's Bureau of Public Affairs undertook to revitalize its methods for keeping the Foreign Service informed about the American public's views on foreign policy issues. As part of this process, I was asked to develop a program for monitoring polls conducted in the United States.

In contrast with a previous State Department program for commissioning surveys, we decided not to do any proprietary polling. Instead, the "American desk" would report on all relevant polls. We would go into much greater depth than the press, but stop short of the elaborate statistical exercises of academic survey research. We would monitor the national polls and the major state polls, assemble the germane questions and responses, acquire supplementary cross-tabulations and demographic break-downs, review trends, compare poll responses, assess the implications of the findings, and then present the assessments on a continuing basis to Department officials.

At the time we began this assignment, the Bureau of Public Affairs was planning a series of "town meetings" on basic foreign policy concerns to be held in various U.S. cities. I suggested that it would be interesting to compare the views expressed by those attending the meetings with the views of random samples of the residents of the town meeting cities. As it turned out, the meetings were held from Pittsburgh to Los Angeles during 1976-1977, cosponsored by the Department and local foreign policy organizations. The polls taken before each meeting were sponsored and underwritten by the Charles F. Kettering Foundation.

These meetings and polls represented a notable departure for a government department with a reputation for aloofness from the public. They were carried out at a time when unique political events had shaken the country, with consequences that were still unmeasured. The fallout from Watergate had not yet settled; a president had resigned; an unelected president was in office; and the Vietnam War was still a raw memory for both hawks and doves. The meetings and polls provided the Department's decision makers with an outline of the foreign policy perceptions, priorities, and concerns of a public that, we soon learned, had become thoroughly disenchanted with Washington.

The chapters that follow offer a concise and cogent discussion of the methodological lessons to be learned from the town-meeting polls and from the stream of national polls on foreign policy issues taken during the past half-dozen years. These lessons are made more instructive by being presented within a broader context than simply how to ask a good poll question. The larger consideration asks how public affairs polls can help decision makers to frame foreign policy.

"They can't be useful, since the public doesn't understand the complexity of our problems," has been a classic response of many policy-making officials. Much of this sniping at polls comes from policy makers who have misapprehended the appropriate role of polls in the overall policy process. Polls, by their very nature, cannot contribute expert knowledge from which to draw technical advice. Random samples of general populations do not extract expertise.

But if those responsible for making and changing policy want to increase the likelihood that their proposals will be adopted, they would be well advised to become sophisticated readers of poll findings. For example, the polls could not tell policy makers how to draft enforceable provisions for a nuclear arms limitation treaty with the Soviet Union. But polls repeatedly told policy makers that the American public's acute distrust of Soviet motives and intentions would focus attention on whether Soviet adherence to such a treaty could be guaranteed. The public debate that took place over the provisions of the SALT II Treaty is the case in point.

Similarly, the polls could not tell policy makers whether the interests of the United States would be well served by a treaty drastically revising the provisions for control and maintenance of the Panama Canal. But the polls did tell policy makers that the public saw no need for such a treaty and was not even acquainted with the concerns that had induced successive administrations, both Democratic and Republican, to continue a painstaking negotiation. That the Panama Canal Treaties were barely ratified after a prolonged debate and last-minute modification is the case in point.

This is not to put all the onus on policy makers who ignore polls. Robinson and Meadow show that the findings of polls on public affairs can be obscure, confusing, contradictory. Polls often fail to turn up instructive findings or, once uncovered, fail to follow them up. On this score, public affairs pollsters share the shortcomings of other political reporters, who also miss stories, report them inadequately, or misread their implications.

It will not do, therefore, simply to exhort policy makers who are non-users to become users. Findings generated by public affairs polls often are not clearly useful to the interested but inexpert policy maker, let alone the jaundiced non-user. That is a condition the following chapters can help to remedy—if the lessons are taken seriously by poll makers concerned about how their findings are utilized by policy makers.

Bernard Roshco
Office of Opinion Analysis
and Plans
Bureau of Public Affairs
U.S. Department of State

Acknowledgments

The authors wish to acknowledge the contributions of several colleagues. John Holm and Dennis Davis provided valuable assistance in the collection of data for the studies in ten major cities. They also helped prepare some early drafts of several chapters.

In later stages of the book's evolution, Percy Tannenbaum, Robert Daley, Stanley Presser, George Bishop, Alvin Richman, and Sam Kernell provided very helpful critiques and suggestions. At a specially convened seminar of Washington policy makers, Davis Bobrow guided the discussion to the points most germane to our study.

Calvin Kytle, president of Seven Locks Press, and editors Simpson Lawson and Ira Brodsky are to be commended for their great patience and editorial skills. Anne Wilson helped edit early drafts of the manuscript.

The perseverance and encouragement of two other individuals were especially crucial. Through his good offices at the Kettering Foundation, Phillips Ruopp provided necessary financial and moral support. It was through his foresight and initiatives at the State Department that Bernard Roshco made this examination of public opinion data possible. While it is appropriate that they are able to express their own viewpoints as prefatory material in the book, the length of their comments does not fairly reflect the extent of their contributions.

Contents

POLLS APART

Introduction

In May, 1979, an NBC News/Associated Press public opinion poll reported that 26 percent of the American public favored the Strategic Arms Limitation Treaty (SALT II) and 7 percent opposed it. The remaining two-thirds of the public, the poll found, did not consider themselves sufficiently informed to have a clear opinion.

Just three days later, an ABC News poll, conducted in the same period by Louis Harris & Associates, Inc., showed 72 percent of the public in favor of the treaty and 18 percent opposed. Only 10 percent in the Harris study were classified in the "don't know" category.

Thus two highly respected polling organizations—organizations with established reputations for determining the state of public opinion within three to five percentage points—differed by approximately 50 percentage points in their descriptions of public opinion on SALT II.

Although divergences of this magnitude are not typical, differences of more than five percentage points were common occurrences in polls on SALT II and other significant foreign policy issues during the past decade, including the Vietnam War, the Middle East, support for the United Nations, the Panama Canal Treaty, and U.S.-Soviet relations. The prevalence of such inconsistencies accounts, in one sense, for the double entendre of our title, *Polls Apart*.

On the pages that follow, we argue that the persistence

of divergences in foreign policy polls severely limits the value of these data for decision makers. We suggest that pollsters can lessen this problem by producing more nearly accurate and complete portrayals of public opinion. For one thing, they can take greater care in framing questions; too often, the kinds of questions they ask impose a frame of reference that makes the expression of opinion considerably less free than it ought to be. Polling organizations can also take steps to see that their characterizations of public opinion distinguish more consistently between the opinions of the uninterested and uninformed and those who understand and care about the issues.

The conventional wisdom holds that public opinion polls have played an increasingly decisive role in much of our recent political history. Poll data are said to have hastened the U.S. withdrawal from Vietnam, helped force the resignation of President Richard Nixon in the aftermath of Watergate, and created political support for increased defense budgets in the 1980s. Those who attribute such influence to the polls cite these examples as evidence that the United States has entered an era of "silent politics," a period in which policy makers let public opinion all but dictate their decisions.

We assess the effect of poll data on foreign policy decision making somewhat differently. We argue that polls on foreign policy operate in a virtual political vacuum. Thus, besides the fact that polls are too frequently apart in their findings, our title is meant to suggest that polls function apart from the workings of the policy process.

In Part I of this book (chapters 1, 2, and 3), we examine the nature and effect of this isolation, drawing from research culled from the scant literature on this subject and from extensive, unstructured discussions with policy makers in the Ford and Carter administrations. Through such inquiry we have been able to outline some reasonably clear patterns of decision making on foreign policy issues and to show how presidents, their chief aides, and legislators use poll data—or fail to use them—in reaching decisions. We have also been able to identify some of the reasons that these patterns are not likely to change soon.

In Part II (chapters 4, 5, 6, and 7), we examine major causes of poll divergences. Chapter 4 presents a detailed documentation of serious divergences on the Panama Canal Treaty, the SALT II Treaty, and other aspects of U.S.-Soviet relations. To show that this need not be the case, we offer in chapter 5 the case history of a series of foreign policy polls conducted in 1976 and 1977 in ten major cities. This project demonstrated that with proper planning and methods, poll findings can converge, and that important differences between mass and elite opinions can be reliably identified and measured. Since major divergences are most likely to occur because of the way poll questions are framed, chapter 6 is devoted to this subject. In chapter 7, we summarize our findings and offer some suggestions about how pollsters can improve the policy relevance of their survey methods.

* * *

Most pollsters have been reluctant to acknowledge that their results often fail to converge on the same portrayal of public opinion. The media—which assiduously report poll data and, increasingly, generate it—fail to call attention to divergent polls. Policy makers rarely discuss the role poll data play in their decisions. Thus there has been no serious debate—certainly no *open* debate—either on the accuracy of polls or the proper use of them in the political process. One of our major purposes is to help generate such a debate.

By way of stating our case, we identify those polling practices that we see as questionable and make recommendations for improving them. We remain mindful, however, that poll findings are only one part of the barrage of influences—facts, claims, petitions, demands—that press on decision makers. We don't presume to tell them how to determine the relative value of opinion-survey results in this spectrum of pressures. The ideas we advance are frankly exploratory. We offer them in the same spirit that moved political scientist Robert Weissberg to explain his rationale for exploring the seemingly imponderable issues surrounding the policy relevance of public opinion in general. "Such issues," he wrote, "are central to the study of public opinion, and to avoid them merely because they do not lend themselves to scientific analysis or because they are unsolvable is to rob the study of public opinion of some of its most fascinating questions."*

John P. Robinson
Robert Meadow

---

*Robert Weissberg, *Public Opinion and Popular Government* (Englewood Cliffs, NJ: Prentice-Hall, Inc., 1976), p. *x*.

PART 1
From Public Opinion to Foreign Policy

1 How Foreign Policy Polls Are Used, Misused, and Ignored

"WHAT WOULD HAVE HAPPENED if Moses had taken a poll in Egypt or if the Israelis had taken a poll among the Palestinians?"[1]

If this rhetorical question by Harry Truman left any doubt about the way he regarded public opinion polls, he made his feelings more explicit on another occasion. "I never paid any attention to the polls myself," he said, "because in my judgment they did not represent a true cross-section of American opinion."[2] Yet barely a decade later, another Democratic president, Lyndon Johnson, was said to carry favorable poll results in his pockets to promote his policies or to refute a critic.[3]

Presidents and their chief aides generally regard public opinion surveys with something between Johnson's infatuation and Truman's cynicism. Given such a wide range of views, we feel it appropriate to ask:

To what degree are national leaders responsive to public opinion in the development of foreign policy? To what degree *should* they respond to public opinion? How well can public opinion polls guide presidents and diplomats in resolving international issues?

The Historical Role of Public Opinion

The proper role of public opinion in society divided political philosophers long before the development of

9

modern polling techniques. Plato considered public deliberation on policy an intrusion on the higher search for order
and wisdom; Aristotle viewed mass opinion as irrational, to
be heeded only if government policies become totally
unacceptable.

In keeping with this classical Greek perspective,
eighteenth century British philosopher Edmund Burke
argued that elected representatives to a legislature should
act as trustees of the public interest rather than delegates
who would merely reflect public opinion. However, as the
concept of the social contract evolved under the influence of
Hobbes, Locke, and Rousseau, the role of public opinion
took on increasing importance. Rousseau went so far as to
describe the law itself as the ultimate expression of community will.

Still, prior to the twentieth century few governments
considered the views of more than a handful of elite citizens.
As Robert Weissberg noted: "Despite attribution of great
power (and sometimes even great practical wisdom) to the
Vox populi, it has not been until relatively recent times that
people have seriously argued that mass sentiment is worthy
of serious political attention."[4]

In America, the idea has had a firmer hold. In fact, some
political theorists have long maintained that the only unique
aspect of the U.S. political system is the degree to which the
public plays a role in self-governance. In 1962, noted
political scholar V.O. Key wrote, "The notion of government by public opinion [flowed] through the history of
American political thought. . . at times thinly, as disillusion-
ment set in; at times in flood, as democratic idealism
flourished."[5]

Key credited Walter Lippmann with helping to deflate the
democratic idealism that pervaded the post-World War I
Progressive era. Lippmann systematically refuted widely
held notions about the capacity of the average man to
govern himself effectively. He argued that the average
person had neither the intellectual ability, training, nor

interest to deal with complex issues of governance, given the time and interest he was compelled to invest in the problems of daily survival. Moreover, he suggested, mass media failed to deliver sufficient information to enable the average person to make crucial decisions. He faulted newspaper editors for conjuring up "phantom publics" by projecting their own viewpoints onto the public at large.

Lippmann wrote: "The private citizen today has come to feel rather like a deaf spectator in the back row who ought to keep his mind on the mystery out there but cannot keep awake."[6] He went on to argue that the majority of the public has no special wisdom and that experts and insiders had far better information on which to make decisions.

Lippmann's views gained credence with time. Subsequent mass movements in other parts of the world in the 1930s, notably communism in the Soviet Union and nazism in Germany, raised suspicions in democratic elite circles about the average citizen's ability to make wise political choices. Concurrently, American advertising's increased ability to create and manipulate public demands for goods and services provided sometimes frightening evidence of how easily public opinion could be molded.

It was during this era of elite pessimism that the scientific public opinion poll was developed, with its attendant claim as an enlightening tool of democracy. Not surprisingly, the technique was met with considerable skepticism among intellectuals and seasoned office holders. They found it inconceivable that citizens so burdened with the problems of day-to-day living could have useful ideas about such domestic issues as taxes, highway construction, or postal service, much less comprehend the dynamics of international treaties or weigh the merits of U.S. intervention in affairs on another continent.

Although this remains a relevant question, scientific opinion sampling has since become a fixture of the political landscape. Beginning in 1940, Princeton University psychology professor Hadley Cantril routinely provided President Roosevelt with poll data on public attitudes about the war in Europe and analyses of them. The fact that Roosevelt's lend-lease proposals withstood the resistance of the isolationists probably should be attributed to careful measurement of public opinion as much as to his legendary sense of political timing.[7]

Subsequent chief executives have found polls similarly useful in manipulating public opinion.[8] Most, however, have been reluctant to acknowledge their reliance on poll data for decision making, presumably because to do so would be at odds with the desired image of a strong president.[9] Ronald Reagan, however, seems to have created his image as a strong leader at least partially because of his careful use of polls. Sidney Blumenthal, writing in the *New York Times Magazine*, suggests that policy polls were used extensively during Reagan's first year in the White House, and perhaps with greater success than in any previous administration.

> Ronald Reagan is governing America by a new strategic doctrine—the permanent campaign. He is applying in the White House the techniques he employed in getting there. Making more effective use of media and market research than any previous President, he has brought into the White House the most sophisticated team of pollsters, media masters and tacticians ever to work there. They have helped him to transcend entrenched institutions like the Congress and the Washington press corps to appeal directly to the people.[10]

Blumenthal believes that the new methods may create new problems for Reagan and his successors (and, no doubt, their pollsters) because "candidates have to deal with shaky coalitions held together by momentary moods, not stable party structures. . . . [and] then must try to govern" as if they were running a "permanent campaign."[11] Whether this strategy will represent greater public input into the policy process or a more subtle form of public manipulation, it is too early to tell.

Current Uses of Public Opinion Data

The political history of the past forty years has amply demonstrated how polls are used by candidates to plot campaign strategies as well as by office holders to keep themselves in office. One might wish that this history also showed a systematic, rational use of poll data in the formation of public policy. The record suggests something else. From our review, we can identify at least three recurrent uses for such polls by policy makers, each use to a considerable degree self-serving.

Polls can identify areas of public apathy, ignorance, or misconception that help policy makers know how best to "inform" the public. The term *inform*, however, usually implies persuasive argument for administration policy rather than academically pure information. President Nixon declared public opinion polls to be useful "only to learn approximately what the people are thinking, so [a politician] ... can talk to them more intelligently."[12] And this view apparently was shared by President Carter. According to his one-time speech writer James Fallows, when polls showed that up to 90 percent of the people opposed ratification of the Panama Canal Treaty, Carter used this as an opportunity to shape arguments that would dispel misunderstandings and misconceptions about the Treaty.[13]

Polls can also provide policy makers with quantifiable public support. When legitimate polls show support for a particular policy, it makes sense that the results be cited. But because of the proliferation of polls and the wide range of variation in framing and presenting questions, surveys taken on the same issue at approximately the same time often yield radically different results, making it possible to find poll results that support any side of an issue. To some extent, politicians should not be blamed for instructing their aides to find a poll that supports policy because they can be certain that their opponents will employ the same strategy.

This selective use of poll data has sometimes led to further abuses, notably the "hired gun" or "loaded" poll—a survey commissioned by a client expressly to establish a point of view. In order to get the desired results, these polls are often conducted with blatant disregard for proper procedure.

Typical of the "hired gun" poll is a telephone survey done by George Fine Research for the Committee on the Present Danger, a group that favored a hard-line position on the SALT II Treaty. Respondents were asked to choose from four position statements the one that best represented their opinion or to indicate that they didn't know enough about the Treaty to have formed an opinion.[14] Three of the four options were negative. Furthermore, one of these negative options provided respondents a convenient means of accepting the committee's assertions that the Treaty would increase U.S. vulnerability to attack. ("I would like to see more protection for the United States before I would be ready to support SALT II.") Of the 71 percent willing to express an opinion, an overwhelming 42 percent chose this option while another 12 percent agreed they would support the Treaty even though they found it "somewhat disappointing." Polling professionals quoted in the *Washington Post*'s report on the findings criticized the question as "loaded" and too complicated to comprehend in a normal telephone interview.

Finally, polls can be used as "trial balloons"; that is, they can identify broad publicly acceptable boundaries in which policy makers may function. Executive branch policy makers may argue that they need isolation from public opinion in order to judge accurately, but they must ultimately reckon with public opinion. Treaties, for example, must be ratified by the Senate, which may be more sensitive to public opinion than the White House. No matter how strong a president's convictions, he cannot continue to press unpopular foreign policy positions without seriously eroding his base of support. Little wonder, then, that foreign policy strategists' interest in public opinion seems to increase as the time approaches for submitting a treaty to the

Senate or for justifying a request for foreign aid before an appropriations committee.

Why Aren't Issue Polls Better Used?

Poll results are playing an increasingly important role in all facets of decision making in Washington. Besides their popularity within the White House, they are being used importantly by executive agencies like the National Security Council and the Department of State. Our research suggests, however, that policy polls are not being used as widely or as well as they could be. This is partly because polls about issues are neither designed carefully enough nor executed in sufficient numbers or with sufficient frequency. Without substantial outside funding, complicated policy studies are infeasible for the national polling organizations, which by and large undertake their own studies as public relations "loss leaders." Issue polls commissioned by the mass media are understandably oriented to the headlines. Few are sponsored by government agencies, for whom such polls would be regarded as self-serving. And academic opinion research is generally lacking in topicality and adequate funding.

But perhaps a more fundamental reason for the underuse and misuse of issue polls lies in the psychology of politicians and policy makers. Politics involves compromise, trade-offs, and deals, activities for which quantitative data are not really needed and are seldom welcomed. Polls on issues therefore are more likely to be relevant only when they seem to suggest how voters would react in the next election to a politician who supported a given policy position.

Policy makers who limit consideration of polling data, or who use it exclusively for the purpose of issue presentation, continue a tradition that characterized leadership before the availability of poll data. There is a need *not* to know about public opinion because it could create potential obstacles that might foreclose certain policy options. Moreover, if a policy maker knows that public opinion does not support his position and he still follows that position, he can be accused of being against "the will of the people." In this event, he would obviously not only shy from quoting the contrary poll data but would use his influence to see that the data got as little publicity as possible.

To explain the use or misuse of poll data by policy makers in any given instance, it is useful to recall the "trustee model" of a legislator advocated by Edmund Burke and the contrasting "delegate model" which holds that legislators should reflect "the voice of the people." With these two models in mind, we can then ask two pertinent questions:

Does the policy maker see accurately measured public opinion data as relevant or appropriate to policy decisions?

Does the policy maker utilize public opinion data?

A policy maker who answers yes to both questions would be one who follows the delegate model; one who answers no to both questions, the trustee model.

Of course, even in these simple categories, there are refinements. A policy maker who believes public opinion is relevant to policy formulation might use the data only to understand the nature of opinion on an issue, to understand the reasons behind those opinions, or to plumb the general intensity of them.

The picture becomes more complicated when we receive a yes-no combination. A policy maker who sees public opinion data as appropriate but does not use them may do so for a number of reasons. The data may be disregarded because the policy maker believes that other factors are more important; in the case of the Panama Canal or SALT treaties, for example, a policy maker may disregard negative public opinion because he or she feels that the treaties are in the best interest of the country.

Potentially, the greatest misuse of polls is caused by the policy maker who does not believe that public opinion data are appropriate to policy formation but who uses them anyway. The danger occurs when the policy maker—citing results from a "hired gun" poll, say—misleads the public with what it wants to hear rather than saying what is true.

One can speculate endlessly on the reasons that policy makers do or do not use poll data, but one should guard against the impulse to assign overly complicated political motives. Often, the reason for not using poll data is quite simple: The data diverge to such a degree that a policy maker who is both honest and busy frankly doesn't know what to make of them. As we shall see in chapter 4, these divergences arise from the fact that pollsters are not as skillful at framing questions as they are at designing statistical samples. Pollsters thus may be inventing their own "phantom publics," different from the specters Walter Lippmann chided editors for creating more than a half century ago, but equally spurious.

Notes

1. Cited by a participant in our roundtable discussion. See chapter 3.
2. Doris A. Graber, *Public Opinion, the President, and Foreign Policy* (New York: Holt, Rinehart and Winston, Inc., 1968), p. 331.
3. Leo Bogart, *Silent Politics* (New York: John Wiley and Sons, Inc., 1972), p. 4.
4. Robert Weissberg, *Public Opinion and Popular Government* (Englewood Cliffs, NJ: Prentice-Hall, Inc., 1976), p. 2.
5. V.O. Key, Jr., *Public Opinion and American Democracy* (New York: Alfred A. Knopf, Inc., 1961), p. 4.
6. Walter Lippmann, *The Phantom Public* (New York: Harcourt Brace, 1925), p. 1.
7. Roosevelt was the first president who had to face the possible tyranny of public opinion polls. Political scientist Frank Cantwell wrote of Roosevelt's plan to pack the Supreme Court despite enormous opposition: "Public opinion in a democracy responds to leadership and needs the stimulus of leadership in order to crystallize one way or another on specific proposals. Public opinion can indicate very powerfully the general area of its needs, but it remains for an individual to come forward with specific proposals toward which public opinion can display approval or disapproval" (Frank Cantwell, "Public Opinion and the Legislative Process," *American Political Science Review* 55[1946]: 935).
8. Theodore Sorenson wrote of President Kennedy's views of public opinion, that "a president has a responsibility to lead public opinion as well as respect it—to shape it, to inform it, to woo it and win it. It can be his sword as well as his

compass." Avoiding the echo chamber character of politics based solely on polls has become problematic for elected officials. "The difference between the old politics and the new politics according to former presidential contender George McGovern is the same as the difference between 'telling people what the public opinion polls say is safe and actually doing what is right for the country'" (Charles W. Roll, Jr. and Albert H. Cantril, *Polls: Their Use and Misuse in Politics* [New York: Basic Books, 1972], p. 40).

9. The extent to which a president acknowledges responsiveness to public opinion raises questions about the degree to which he meets public expectations about his role as a decision maker. Political scientist Roberta Sigel found in her respondents a strong desire for presidential leadership. She often heard responses such as "That is his job" or "That is what we elected him for" and "He knows more than most" when they were asked why a president should do what he feels is best rather than follow public opinion (Roberta Sigel, "Image of the American Presidency—Part II of an Exploration into Popular Views of Presidential Power," *Midwest Journal of Political Science* 10:123-137, passim).

10. Sidney Blumenthal, "Marketing the President," *New York Times Magazine*, 13 September 1981, p. 43.

11. Ibid., p. 118.

12. Roll and Cantril, *Polls*, p. 136.

13. Albert Cantril, ed., *Polling on the Issues* (Cabin John, MD: Seven Locks Press, 1980), p. 135.

14. The exact question and the optional responses:

The United States is now negotiating a strategic arms agreement with the Soviet Union in what is known as "SALT TWO." Which *ONE* of the following statements is closest to your opinion on these negotiations:

— I strongly support SALT II	8%
— SALT II is somewhat disappointing, but on balance, I would have to support it.	12%
— I would like to see more protection for the United States before I would be ready to support SALT II.	42%
— I strongly oppose the SALT arms agreement with the Russians.	9%
— (I don't know enough about the SALT II Treaty to have formed an opinion yet).	29%
	100%

2 *Problems with Polls*

"JUDGING FROM THE PROLIFERATION of polls of public opinion, there appears to be no limit on the number of times attitudes can be numbered, sorted, and analyzed."[1]

The seeming absence of limits on public opinion polling, noted by this *New York Times* writer early in the 1980 presidential campaign, tends to obscure the clear limits that exist on the uses to which poll findings can be put. The proliferation of polls does attest to their value for anticipating the preferences of both consumers and voters. As one of the staples in the "new politics," polls have come to be regarded by office seekers as indispensable in formulating campaign strategies. Polls also are clearly of value when used by the media to provide insights into what citizens are thinking; they have thus become a fashionable, and presumably more credible, way for journalists to do what has always been one of their major functions, which is to monitor what is happening in the society.[2]

But when the mass media report results of polls on issues, there is the implicit expectation that public officials *ought* to be responsive—almost as if poll results represent a public referendum. The expectation is unrealistic. An issue poll differs from a true referendum in at least two important particulars: Poll results are not legally binding, and the numbers and types of people participating in polls and referenda are so dissimilar as to defy comparison. Furthermore—as presently designed, conducted, and reported—

issue polls make it virtually impossible for even the most obliging public officials to respond with either the immediacy or the wisdom that the media and the populists among us apparently want them to.

Even the most disciplined and refined issue polls are difficult to translate into decision-making terms, and as long as this condition prevails such polls will be of only peripheral value to policy makers. The problems are legion. Some of the problems can be attributed to the circumstances under which polls are conducted and made public. Others, as we will say many times in this book, derive from the ambiguities and shallowness of the opinions that have been ostensibly measured and codified. Still others are inherent in the nature of the policy-formation process itself.

Timing Problems

On matters of foreign policy, it is particularly difficult to collect accurate and useful opinion data, and perhaps even more difficult to present them in a decision-making context. International events break so rapidly that there is seldom time for solid assessment of policy opinions. While "overnight" poll results can be obtained, their validity is questionable. Have the poll respondents had access to and assimilated sufficient information to meaningfully evaluate a foreign policy crisis? Have they taken into account the complex underlying problems that created the crisis?

While polls about noncrisis decisions give officials greater opportunity to analyze public opinion data, they also present problems. A policy or piece of legislation under consideration may not be covered very closely in the mass media prior to the actual vote or decision. By and large, polls under such circumstances can reveal only that the public is ignorant on the issue, hardly a helpful discovery for a well-intentioned policy maker.

Poll data also lose their significance when too much time elapses between research design and its publication. This is a particular problem of analyses by academic researchers. While analysts of public opinion data at academic centers—such as the University of Michigan, Stanford University, or the University of Chicago—reach for a deeper understanding of public opinion than commercial pollsters, academicians may require years instead of months or weeks to complete their work. Few policy makers have the luxury of this much time, even when formulating general policy.

Poll Questions Oversimplify Issues

Most commercial polls must reduce complex foreign policy questions into short, simple statements to which respondents are expected to agree or disagree. These brief statements invariably oversimplify the issues. The problem is compounded when issue questions are piggy-backed or caravaned on omnibus surveys containing a range of questions (including questions pertaining to product marketing). Unsolicited comments are not encouraged and open-ended questions are rare because of the increased cost of coding responses to them. Because these questions merely summarize the pro-con opinions on complex issues, they offer decision makers only general and superficial readings of policy preferences.[3] As one foreign policy maker, Adam Yarmolinsky, put it almost twenty years ago:

> There are surprisingly few operationally significant questions for the policy maker as to which any public opinion, in my view, exists at all. By an operationally significant question, I mean a question the answer to which will affect specific actions of government officials. The overwhelming bulk of these questions are of means and not of ends.[4]

Thus, in the early emotional days of the Iranian hostage crisis, what could a policy maker do when faced with simple approval or disapproval of how he was handling the situation? The situation was too complex. Polling data can be translated into action only when the issues are well defined and the policy alternatives clearly spelled out. Moreover, few polls can afford to indicate which policies are preferred, given the various costs involved. Consider the difficulty, for example, of framing a series of questions that would indicate what price the public would be willing to pay—in lives, money, or international prestige—for direct intervention in another country.

Other question framing problems occur when pollsters use such abstractions as "detente" and such acronyms as "SALT II" and "MX weapons." Respondents who don't fully understand the terms are forced to either make an uncertain choice or acknowledge their ignorance, something few poll respondents seem comfortable admitting. Hence polls typically fail to distinguish the responses of those who understand and have formed opinions on an issue from those whose understanding is minimal and who hold no firm position. This further contributes to the kind of "study which purports to show the will of the people but which, in fact, is merely a whim of the people."[5]

The Need for Multiple Questions

For policy makers to gain a clear understanding of public opinion, they have to study each issue from a variety of perspectives. To be truly useful, therefore, pollsters should specify the limited (or varied) aspects of the issue they're examining. As survey methodologists Howard Schuman and Stanley Presser concluded in their recent, comprehensive research into the effects of question wording:

> ... it is dangerous to work with single items on any important issue. Enough question effects have been discovered to indicate that conclusions based on a single item may be influenced in unexpected ways. Since the influence tends to occur in unanticipated directions, several items in *different forms, wordings*, and *contexts* will ordinarily greatly reduce the danger.[6]

A classic divergence due to different ways of asking what appeared to be the same question arose in 1944. One poll reported a majority favored a proposed constitutional amendment limiting the president to two terms. A second showed a majority intended to vote for President Roosevelt for a fourth term. Similarly, foreign policy polls find respondents supporting policies once they are adopted, even though they opposed them before they were put into action.

Opinions Differ from Behavior

Another factor limiting the use of opinion polls for policy purposes has to do with the common disparity between opinion and conviction. One can count on this disparity even on the most salient of issues, like those touching on the state of the economy or war and peace. Foreign policy makers especially have no real cause to fear public opinion, and only rarely do they have reason to respect it. For polls reflect only what people say, not what they will do. Even those few respondents who are both concerned and informed about an issue will not necessarily act on their opinions by writing letters, withholding taxes, or trying to recall leaders. In other words, opinion is only a "soft" indicator of behavior.

This link between opinion and behavior is further weakened when issue positions are described in abstract or hypothetical terms. Indeed it has been shown that questions about concrete situations show different results than abstract questions on the same basic principle. In their well-known study of public opinion in 1960, Prothro and Grigg found far more people agreed with democratic principles in the abstract (e.g., free speech) than their application in specific situations (e.g., free speech on an unpopular issue like communism).[7] How can policy makers act on opinions whose foundations are so tenuous, unstable, and unrelated to concrete political behavior?

Polls and Democracy

The mass media play an indispensable role in both

bringing soundings of public opinion to the attention of foreign policy makers and establishing the legitimacy of these data to the policy process.[8] But once reported, poll data enter a very dense stream of potential policy guidance, and policy makers must pay attention to these other sources as well. Depending on where they sit in the policy-making sequence, these sources include political actors of varying but impressive powers—members of the executive and legislative branches, members of the permanent bureaucracy at agencies like the State Department and the CIA, foreign diplomats, international representatives of business and banking, and many other interest groups affected by specific policies. In this kind of policy setting, poll data must be very clear and decisive to be persuasive. They rarely are.

But beyond the technical and procedural limitations, we face a greater and more fundamental obstacle to the proper use of issue polls. Before we can make polls work better, we have to decide what job we want them to do.

The proper relationship between a democracy and public opinion remains a complicated question.[9] Elections may be held too infrequently for the public to have control over their elected representatives, and elections provide virtually no control over appointed officials. Examples can be found of policy makers who are too comfortably removed from the heat of public opinion to have the public's interest at heart. We do expect varying responses to public opinion due to the diversity of political actors and roles, differences in issues and time constraints, and so forth. But the wide range of variation from instance to instance suggests that policy makers have not defined any ground rules about how public opinion polls should be used.

In chapter 1, we noted some of the ways that polls can serve other goals in the policy process: revealing levels of public ignorance and confusion and allowing policy makers to deflate public expectations or heighten awareness of policies. Like other "trial balloons," poll findings can help decision makers anticipate public opposition. But if they are going to be used merely to help officials push their own positions, polls become little more than propaganda tools. Polling becomes a one-way communication channel that only exploits the good will of the public. We think that two-way communication could begin if policy makers explained why they have used or disregarded opinion data in each case. Failing this, it would seem appropriate for pollsters to learn more about what actually happens to the information that the public has entrusted to them.

Policy makers, journalists, pollsters, political scientists, and the general public will not easily—may not ever—agree on the proper use of public opinion. But the most constructive reforms of the polling process will have to follow some agreement about what we as a nation want public opinion polls to accomplish.

Notes

1. E.J. Dionne, "1980 Brings More Pollsters Than Ever," *New York Times*, 16 February 1980, p. 10.

2. Albert Gollin, "Exploring the Liaison between Polling and the Press," *Public Opinion Quarterly* 44(1980): 447-448.

3. Moreover, when pollsters simplify issues, they may also change and shape the structure of elite political debate on that issue. As we note in chapter 4, poll data on the Panama Canal Treaty restricted discussion to those dimensions of the issue examined by the polls, particularly in reference to the Treaty as a "giveaway" of the Canal. See also Roshco, 1978.

4. Adam Yarmolinsky, "Confessions of a Non-User," *Public Opinion Quarterly* 27(1963): 543.

5. Mervin D. Field, "Public Polls and the Public Interest" in *Polling on the Issues*, Albert H. Cantril, ed. (Cabin John, MD: Seven Locks Press, 1980), p. 184.

6. Howard Schuman and Stanley Presser, *Questions and Answers in Attitude Surveys: Experiments on Question Form, Wording and Context* (New York: Academic Press, Inc., 1981), p. 312.

7. James Prothro and Charles Grigg, "Fundamental Principles of Democracy: Bases of Agreement and Disagreement," *Journal of Politics* 22(1960): 276-294.

8. A recent symposium on polls and the news media identified several main reasons for the proliferation of polls: a concern for precision journalism, more sophisticated reporting, and new angles on the news (Gollin, 1980). To some extent, there is a contagion effect, with journalists feeling they must conduct polls to remain competitive. Unfortunately, the resulting expansion of polls has not been accompanied by a critical look at how public opinion polls could best be used.

9. There is little tradition and no constitutional mandate for the application of poll data to the policy process. In fact, our country's leaders determined policy for the first 160 years of the republic without any public opinion poll data. As a result, no rules and few traditions have evolved for giving public opinion data consideration in decision making. As Robert Weissberg succinctly argued: "The American constitutional system can be characterized as a 'stacked deck' against the accurate translation of popular preferences into policy. Both constitutional history and present institutional structure strongly suggest that governing in accord with pressing mass desires has been a relatively low priority for leaders" (Weissberg, *Public Opinion and Popular Government*, p. 249).

3 *The Making and Selling of Foreign Policy*

"I don't know of any case in which anyone makes policy because public opinion tells them such a policy is necessary."

THIS COMMENT APTLY SUMMARIZES the views of about thirty government policy makers whom we consulted in an effort to find out how polls are actually used in the conduct of foreign policy. We solicited such views in two ways. At the time of the Carter-Reagan transition, we held a four-hour long seminar, attended by some fifteen people, including members of the White House staff and the National Security Council in the Ford and Carter administrations; career officers in the State and Defense departments; and representatives of key congressional committees that deal with foreign policy. We conducted individual interviews with a like number of Washington policy makers who could not attend the seminar. To encourage complete candor from all participants, we agreed not to identify them in this book.

From the recollections of our seminar participants and interviewees we traced this recurring theme: although only limited use is made of public opinion data in *policy formulation,* such data are often carefully analyzed when officials plan *presentation* of their policies to the public.

The Executive Branch

We opened the seminar by asking the participants to comment on a 1963 article by Adam Yarmolinsky, a special assistant to the secretary of defense during the Kennedy administration. Yarmolinsky described polls as being used "less to discover the state of public opinion on a topic than to try to find a way to make clear why the government had chosen a particular course of action."[1]

On this and other issues, our informants' responses differed, depending on whether they had served in the executive or the legislative branches, or on whether they were appointees or career employees. Not surprisingly, those in the executive branch described their agencies as less responsive to poll data and public influence than those in the legislative branch. Two former staff members of the National Security Council in the Carter administration claimed they could not recall a single instance when public opinion data were even cited during policy deliberations, including those involving the Panama Canal Treaty, which the administration knew would require Senate ratification.

The insulation that career status provides became apparent early in the discussion. A White House staff member described certain ranking career officials in the State and Defense departments as essentially "above all this concern with public opinion." Others implied that these policy makers simply dismissed the significance of public opinion when it was perceived as unfavorable to the goals of their agencies. An official of one agency whose policies had consistently failed to gain enthusiastic public support in the polls said he and his colleagues had "essentially written off the public."

Former White House staff members acknowledged that on occasions they also disregarded poll data. For example, ample public opinion data on the Panama Canal and SALT II treaties revealed substantial public resistance to the provisions of those treaties even as they were being negotiated.

One informant suggested that the Carter White House misinterpreted poll data on SALT II because "public opinion data on SALT were filtered through the perception [by presidential aides] of what the public *ought to* think." (Emphasis ours.) Others suggested that long-range planning data, such as those compiled at the State Department, made little impact on a White House staff who had their hands full taking care of each day's problems. Anticipating possible problems six or twelve months down the road was viewed as a luxury they couldn't afford.

Preoccupation with current crises also appears to make policy makers susceptible to the standard principles of selective perception, according to one observer.

> [Policy makers] were warned that the Panama Canal Treaty would be a hassle to pass, but they did not want to believe it. They were warned that SALT would be a tough one to pass, but they did not want to believe it. They were warned that the domestic incursion of refugees [from Vietnam] would create problems, but they did not want to believe it. Policy makers are only concerned with the market research that is ultimately political and requisite for the enactment of their policies. . . . Only when it comes before Congress do the Panama negotiators or the SALT people worry about how the people feel.

> What the policy maker prefers to do when he gets the "wrong" answer, is tell you how bad the questions are. . . . He doesn't want to know what runs contrary to his predilections.

Experiences in the policy councils had taught our informants that not all crises are equal.

> On major policy questions, the president does not try to choose a course of action which he knows the public won't accept. That's a basic tenet of foreign policy deliberations. He may occasionally go against the flow, and he might do it on the Panama Canal issue, which is not an overriding issue of survival or destruction. But the SALT issue *is,* and they don't go against the public's wishes [on such issues].

Casual attitudes toward public opinion during the intramural deliberations and staff debate have a way of changing once the president or secretary of state gives his blessing to a policy. Then the policy makers strongly feel the need to know "what to educate the public about," as one National Security Agency aide put it. It is at this point that poll data can be particularly useful and when they are in most demand.

Poll findings become valuable guides for speech writers and others responsible for presenting the rationale for administration policies. One former presidential speech writer, James Fallows, has spoken and written extensively of his experiences with the Carter administration.

> The polling data I usually saw in the government were connected with the *salesmanship* of a program as opposed to the development of its policy.[2]

Some of the reported disregard for poll findings during policy deliberations in the Carter White House may be accounted for by Fallows's statement that "if it came to a choice between doing what he [Carter] thought was right (with a capital R) and what people would approve in the polls, he would instantly choose the Right."

> Polling data are useful to the extent that they tell you *how* to do things you have already decided to do for other reasons, and they are potentially damaging and destructive to the extent that they take the place of other ways of deciding *what* you want to do.[3]

The same polls that provide insights for adminstration spokespersons provide "ammunition" for the administration's opponents.[4] Presidents and their aides often feel compelled to counteract the effect of an unfavorable poll in the way they would a critical editorial in an influential publication or a critical statement by a well-known public figure.

Public officials recognize that the media, once resistant to polls, have now embraced them. These officials often feel that efforts to compress findings into tightly edited articles or newscasts result in oversimplification, if not distortion. One of our roundtable participants felt that because the media had described an early version of the Panama Canal Treaty as a "give-away," the Carter administration had a tough time proving that the treaty was an economically feasible and rational step toward improved U.S. relations with Third World nations.

In summary, public opinion data are used in the executive branch primarily to indicate, as one official said, "where the public ought to go." Knowledge of what the public believes and wants to hear can help politicians make convincing presentations of their policies. In the words of one of our informants, the purpose of examining poll data is to determine "how you can sell a policy that you think is right."

The Congress

Legislators, particularly those approaching reelection, tend to be more sensitive to public opinion than appointed administrators or career employees. As one of our roundtable discussants said, constituents remember when their representatives disagree with them, not when they agree. During a representative's or senator's term of office, a coalition of constituents discontented with the handling of single issues can emerge to create electoral problems. "A senator can only afford to be a diplomat once every six years," one Senate aide told us. "The closer you come to an election," said another, "the harder it is to brush up against public opinion."

The intensity of a legislator's commitment to an issue often determines how much attention he or she pays to poll results. One Senate aide indicated that polls do not matter when a senator feels strongly on a question. However, as in the executive branch, polls can help a senator clarify his position. When a legislator feels less strongly, however, poll support for an issue may sway a fence-straddling legislator.

Perhaps the most unreliable indicators of public opinion are the polls legislators conduct of their constituents. More often than not, these congressional polls merely serve to explain or justify policy choices. Most tend to be symbolic and ritualistic appeals for voting "instructions." Given the methodology employed in congressional polls, legislators might be better advised to ignore their results.[5] Consider this question from a 1972 congressional survey:

> Do you feel demonstrators who block U.S. troop trains, burn draft cards, and send blood to North Vietnam should be fined and imprisoned when such acts would be considered treasonous if we were in a declared state of war?[6]

This emotional question betrays the attitude of the designer and distorts the issue since the U.S. was not in a declared state of war.[7]

One senator's aide told us of an independent poll his boss commissioned to determine public reaction to a version of the Panama Canal Treaty that incorporated amendments he favored. The results of this poll were just as the senator had hoped: public rejection of the Treaty as originally negotiated but public support for a treaty hypothetically revised to reflect his amendments. While there was no certainty that the results would turn out as the senator had hoped, he could have just as conveniently decided not to publish the results if they were not so favorable. In this case, the data from the private poll helped develop a congressional consensus of support for the amendments.

Finally, members of Congress sometimes encounter polls used as threats by various interest groups. Poorly conducted polls by some groups may receive legitimate treatment by the media in the congressman's district. Our discussants indicated that on more than one occasion legislators have been compelled to keep a low profile on issues when their positions deviated from those the media attributed to their constituents, lest they be seen as voting against public opinion.

There are some developments that have ensured that polls are being more carefully considered in Congress. A regular office devoted to providing legislators and committee staffs with public opinion data has been established within the Congressional Research Service (CRS). Although the CRS does not conduct polls, it does have access to a wide range of poll data and offers professional evaluations of the quality and meaning of survey data. The service is widely used and is apparently in increasing demand by members of Congress, although the demand is far short of universal. It encourages members to examine poll data, even when the data do not support their positions. Nonetheless, there was clear evidence in the case of the Panama Canal Treaty, for example, that both sides were able to find polls to support their positions.

Foreign Policy Polls Today

Throughout our discussion, it became clear that no systematic procedures or norms had developed for the introduction of poll data into the political process. On occasion, policies have even been adapted to avoid polling data, as in the case of the executive agency with consistently meagre public support. In general, our discussants said they did not consider polls in policy formulation because of a combination of philosophical and technical problems with them. Some argued that leaders would be paralyzed if they followed polls closely during the policy-formulation process.

On the other hand, polls were acknowledged to be useful as a reference to the public's general political intelligence, and even more as an index to the gaps in public understanding on specific issues. Furthermore, American poll data are apparently often cited effectively during negotiations with other countries. For example, chief American negotiator Paul Warnke of the Arms Control and Disarmament Agency during the Carter administration described how poll data were used in SALT II negotiations to explain objectively to his Soviet counterparts the limited concessions the American public was willing to make. Warnke also used these data to keep himself informed about how successful the administration was in persuading the public of the wisdom of its negotiation policies.[8] Our informants described how polls played a similar role in Canal Treaty negotiations.

But uses of public opinion data have also—perhaps originally—been used by other countries. German chancellor Konrad Adenauer, for example, was said to have skillfully used German public opinion data to extract concessions from American officials overseeing the rebuilding of Germany after World War II.

Today, the U.S. International Communications Agency systematically collects public opinion data in other countries. These are used by presidents in preparing statements and speeches addressing the concerns of citizens of other countries during official visits. The reverse process holds as well: Policy makers in other countries consult data on American public opinion to plan and negotiate with their American counterparts.

Ironically, this may constitute the best example of how American public opinion can play a proper role in policy deliberation. In time, it may lead our policy makers to pay greater attention to the voice of public opinion as reflected in poll results.

Notes

1. Yarmolinsky, "Confessions of a Non-User," p. 547.

2. Albert H. Cantril, ed., *Polling on the Issues* (Cabin John, MD: Seven Locks Press, 1980), p. 134.

In the first months of the Reagan administration much the same "sales mentality" about public opinion was evident. Author Sidney Blumenthal quotes a White House pollster regarding the unfavorable public opinion about administration policy on El Salvador: "What was wrong with El Salvador was the packaging of the activity, in terms of policy and presentation to the public. It wasn't well staged or sequenced" (Blumenthal, "Marketing the President," p. 112).

3. Cantril, *Polling on the Issues*, pp. 134-135.

4. As Richard Nixon stated during his Watergate crisis, "I don't give one damn what the polls say insofar as affecting my decisions. I only care about them because they affect my ability to lead" (Richard Nixon, *The Memoirs of Richard Nixon* [New York: Grosset and Dunlop, 1978], p. 753).

5. Marascuilo and Amster (1964) studied the methodologies of the polls of ninety-five representatives and four senators—and found wide variation in the populations sampled. In some cases, questionnaires were sent only to those requesting one and few tallies were made of either the number sent or the number returned.

6. Bogart, *Silent Politics*, p. 5.

7. More recent legislative questionnaires show little sign of improvement. One senator from a Northeastern industrial state recently asked those on his mailing list the following question:

"Which of the following statements best describes your feelings towards present U.S. policy in the Mideast?

1. The U.S. is siding too much with Israel.
2. The U.S. is siding too much with the Arabs."

The question forces respondents to take an extreme position, excluding more realistic options, such as "the right amount." Moreover, knowing whether the voters felt that the U.S. was *not* siding enough with either the Israelis or Arabs would have been more instructive to the senator. Finally, constituents' answers would probably have varied greatly if particular Arab countries had been named.

8. Cantril, *Polling on the Issues*, p. 143.

PART 2
How Polls Work

4 *Divergences on Four Foreign Policy Issues*

WHEN POLLING ORGANIZATIONS release their findings to the public or the media, it is now standard practice to acknowledge that the results are subject to discrepancy due to sampling errors. The possibility of such errors is increasingly mentioned by the news media—a notable improvement in poll data reporting.

Scant attention is paid, however, to discrepancies in the findings of major polling organizations on the same issue. Yet it is these divergences, to a far greater degree than those caused by statistical error, that should lead policy makers and the public to be skeptical of poll data. As we saw in the introduction, while one major polling organization showed 26 percent support for the SALT II Treaty, another organization—interviewing the same types of people chosen to be representative of the public and at the same time—indicated 72 percent support. There were also serious contradictions in polls on other leading foreign policy issues of the 1970s—the Panama Canal Treaty, U.S.-Soviet relations, support for the United Nations, and defense spending. A succession of scholars has identified the discrepant portrayals of public opinion on such foreign policy issues as Vietnam (Converse and Schuman, 1969); the Middle East (Lipset, 1976); and the Panama Canal (Roshco, 1979). Despite this, there is little apparent recognition of their implications by policy makers, pollsters, or the public. Few mass media analysts lay polls on issues side-by-side for careful comparison.

This is in marked contrast to the critical publicity given to divergences in poll results on elections. The differences between poll projections and reality are immediately obvious to everyone when the polls project different winners in an election or when they fail to predict the winner. Gallup's poll projection of a Dewey victory over Truman in 1948, although off by only 5 percentage points, was subjected to national ridicule.

Of course, one cannot expect the same degree of predictability to apply to opinion polls on issues. Public opinions on issues are less sharply focused and change more frequently than opinions on candidates. Party loyalties are less of a factor in respondents' replies to issue polls, and their answers are more likely to be shaped by short-term emotional factors and the media information they are exposed to. Poll data on issues must, therefore, be judged by different standards than those used in political polling.

The serious questions that have been raised about "non-sampling" errors in books, articles, and professional journals have more serious implications for issue polling than for voter-preference polls.[1] Sources of nonsampling errors can include the method of interviewing used, the way questions are worded, and the format or order of questions asked in the questionnaire. The following examples of inconsistent foreign policy poll results defy explanation in terms of error due to sampling:

- In the January-February period of 1978, a Gallup poll found 37 percent opposition to the Panama Canal Treaty, a CBS poll found 51 percent opposition, and an Opinion Research Corporation poll found 78 percent opposition.[2]
- A national survey given in May 1977 contained three questions designed to measure public support of the United Nations. One question showed 32 percent

public support of the U.N.; another showed 47 percent support; and the last showed 74 percent support.[3]

- Four rather different questions in a 1974-75 Louis Harris/ABC News survey each indicated that two-thirds of the public supported military aid to Israel; yet a poll by Yankelovich, Skelly & White done at almost the same time found that only 31 percent felt the U.S. should send arms to Israel (with 57 percent opposed).[4]
- In the same 1974-75 survey, three apparently similar questions showed that 11, 25, and 36 percent of the public, respectively, agreed that Israel should return the Palestinian land occupied since the 1967 war.[5]
- Almost a third of a national sample (30 percent) expressed an opinion on the Agricultural Trade Act, obscure legislation that few members of the public would have occasion to hear about.[6]

All these inconsistencies suggest that in the reporting of results pollsters need to move beyond their present standard disclaimers about sampling errors. Variations that occur when different polling organizations ask what appear to be similar questions but get different results must be brought to the public's attention. Not only do findings diverge, but interpretation of them sometimes engenders conflict among pollsters. Pollster Burns Roper took exception to a 1979 *U.S. News and World Report* statement that "opinion polls indicate overwhelming public support for SALT II," by noting that "at no time has *Roper Reports* found more than 42 percent favoring passage." His comments were in turn criticized by Warren Mitofsky, the director of the CBS Election Survey Unit, who argued that the "*Roper Reports'* negative findings about the new SALT II Treaty were due to one sentence in the [Roper] introduction. I reject the notion that any one of the polls is right or wrong, as you imply in your [Roper's] conclusion. It is more reasonable to believe that they are merely different."[7]

The widespread divergences of polls on four foreign policy

issues included in the above catalog of problems will be given closer examination in this chapter. These issues are the SALT II and Panama Canal treaties, U.S.-Soviet relations, the United Nations.

Overall, we find that the most dramatically different portrayals of public opinion regularly occur between responses to "filtered" and "unfiltered" questions. Most poll questions are unfiltered. An interviewer asks a direct question and if respondent is uncertain or has no fixed opinion on the topic, he or she must volunteer a "no opinion" response. A filtered question lets respondents avoid a direct reply without having to reveal their lack of awareness or conviction. A typical filtered question might end with such a phrase as ". . . or haven't you thought about this enough to have an opinion one way or the other?"

Recent experimental evidence shows that 10-20 percent of the public will make use of the filter when it is offered. As we noted in our introduction, more than 50 percent of the respondents to the question about SALT II used it.

SALT II

From the time it was negotiated in 1977 until it was crowded off the diplomatic agenda by the 1979 Soviet invasion of Afghanistan, the SALT II Treaty was the object of almost fifty separate polling assessments. Some of the questions that were repeated most often across time are arranged in Tables 1 and 2. While one of the poll readings extends as far back as 1975, most questions were asked in 1977, 1978, and 1979 when passage of the Treaty seemed likely. Extensive surveying has been done on this issue with both filtered and unfiltered poll questions.

The first part of Table 1 shows the results of three unfiltered poll questions on U.S.-Soviet nuclear arms limitation, conducted by three different polling organizations over an extended period of time. NBC/Associated Press, Louis Harris/ABC News, and CBS News/*N.Y.*

Times clearly showed support for the general idea of the Treaty, by margins ranging from 2-to-1 to 8-to-1, depending on the date of the survey. In the spring of 1979, the three organizations' questions can be shown to have produced a significant similarity: a 68 percent to 22 percent margin for a March NBC/AP poll, a 72 percent to 18 percent margin for a May Harris/ABC poll, and a 77 percent to 15 percent margin for CBS News/*N.Y. Times* in June. However, while NBC/AP and Harris/ABC indicated a period of declining support compared to earlier surveys, CBS/*N.Y. Times* indicated some increase in support, although differently phrased questions were employed by CBS/*N.Y. Times* in late 1978 and early 1979.[8]

With the introduction of a "filter," however, major differences in findings became evident. In the case of the NBC/AP question, between 79 percent (in March 1979) and 44 percent (in October 1979) took advantage of the filter option to say that they had no fixed opinion on the topic. In a 1977-78 survey by the Roper Organization, about 30 percent of the respondents chose the filter option. Until July 1979, both the NBC/AP and the Roper filtered questions still indicated at least 2-to-1 public support for the Treaty, closely paralleling the balance of opinion suggested by the unfiltered question.

Once again, however, the polls diverge concerning the date and extent of the 1979 swing in public opinion. The NBC/AP filtered question showed a significant shift from a 26-7 percent margin in May to a 21-17 percent margin in July. Recalculated on "opinion-only" basis, support shifted from 85 percent in May to 55 percent in July (and it can be seen that the margin had become less than 50 percent by September). Yet NBC/AP's unfiltered question registered only a mild 3 percentage point decline (from 68 percent to 65 percent) over the longer April-July period. To be sure, the questions are framed differently. While the filtered question refers directly to the SALT II Treaty, the unfiltered question refers only to the idea of a treaty. It is clear that the two questions are sensitive to different events and different circumstances. While the differences in question format seem obvious in retrospect, they are seldom so apparent when pollsters are deciding what question to put on a survey or how to report the results to the public. When the emphasis is on reporting balances and trends in opinion with single numbers, the fact that different questions produce different results becomes of secondary interest.

The Gallup filtered question in Table 2 produced very similar shift patterns across the March-June 1979 period (from a 27-9 percent March pro-con edge to a 34-19 percent June margin) to the NBC/AP filtered question in Table 1 across the May-July period of that year (from 26-7 percent in May to 21-17 percent in July). However, the CBS/*Times* filtered question in Table 2 for June of 1979 produced a 27-9 percent margin, which was more similar to March and May readings of Gallup and NBC/AP.

TABLE 1

ATTITUDES TOWARD SALT AGREEMENTS WITH SOVIET UNION

Unfiltered Questions

NBC News/Associated Press: "Do you favor or oppose a new agreement between the United States and Russia which would limit nuclear weapons?"

	1978					1979				
	JAN.	JUNE	AUG.	OCT.	NOV.	JAN.	MAR.	APR.	JULY	SEPT.
Favor	74%	67%	71%	70%	75%	81%	71%	68%	65%	62%
Oppose	19	22	22	21	17	14	18	22	25	30
Don't Know	7	11	7	9	8	5	11	10	10	8

Louis Harris/ABC News: "Would you favor or oppose the U.S. and Russia coming to a new SALT arms agreement?"

	1975	1977	1978			1979		
	DEC.	MAR.	MAY	MAY	JUNE	JAN.	APR.	MAY
Favor	59%	66%	77%	74%	72%	74%	75%	72%
Oppose	14	8	8	12	17	16	14	18
Don't Know	27	26	14	13	11	10	11	10

CBS News/ *N.Y. Times*: "Do you favor or oppose the United States and Russia coming to an agreement to limit nuclear weapons?"

	1977	1978			1979	
	APR.*	JUNE	NOV.*	DEC.*	JAN.*	JUNE
Favor	71%	78%	65%	63%	63%	77%
Oppose	19	14	28	24	26	15
Don't Know	10	8	7	13	11	8

*Different question wording:

> April and December: "Do you think the United States should or should not negotiate a treaty with the Russians to cut back military weapons?"
>
> November: "Would you favor or oppose an agreement with Russia limiting military weapons?"
>
> January: "Do you think the United States should or should not negotiate a treaty to limit strategic military weapons?"

Filtered Questions

NBC News/ Associated Press: "At the present time, the United States and the Soviet Union are close to reaching agreement on a new Strategic Arms Limitation Agreement, usually called SALT II. Have you heard or read enough about it to have an opinion? (If yes,) Do you favor or oppose the new SALT agreement?"

	1979				
	MAR.	MAY	JULY	SEPT.	OCT.
Favor	13%	26%	21%	20%	25%
Oppose	6	7	17	23	26
Not sure	2	3	4	3	5
Haven't heard or read enough	79	64	58	54	44

The Roper Organization: "The United States and Russia are trying to come to a new agreement limiting each country's nuclear weapons. This agreement would replace the Strategic Arms Limitation Treaty, called SALT, that ran out last October. Are you in favor of, or opposed to, signing a new SALT agreement with Russia, or haven't you been paying much attention to this issue?"

	1977	1978	
	NOV.	JUNE	AUG.
Favor	43%	45%	41%
Oppose	10	11	16
No attention	29	30	29
Depends	8	6	8

The situation is somewhat clarified by the Roper Organization's unfiltered question in Table 2, which does show a shift in the pro-con margin from 9 percentage points (33-24 percent) in May to 2 points in July (31-29 percent). However that shift is far less than the 19 point difference (40-21 percent) that the question elicited between January of 1979 and May of 1979. While a similar decline in support during early 1979 is supported by the NBC/AP unfiltered question in Table 1, it is not shown by either the Harris/ABC unfiltered question or the NBC/AP filtered question.

Moreover, while the polls did converge on the finding that support had significantly wavered by the fall of 1979, they diverged on the extent of the general pro-con split.[9] Responses varied from a 5 point pro advantage (CBS/ *Times* filtered [25-20 percent] and Harris unfiltered [42-37 percent]) through a 2-3 point con advantage (NBC/AP filtered [20-23 percent] and Gallup filtered [24-26 percent]) to a 9 point con advantage (Roper unfiltered [30-39 percent]). While it may be argued that all those polls reflected a close vote on this issue, one is still left with the impression of greater divergence that would be useful for clear policy direction.

TABLE 2

ATTITUDES TOWARD (SENATE) RATIFICATION OF SALT II TREATY

Filtered Questions

CBS News/*N.Y. Times*: "The Senate will debate the U.S. treaty with the Soviet Union which limits strategic nuclear weapons—called SALT. From what you know about this treaty, do you think the Senate should vote for or against it, or don't you know enough about it to have an opinion?"

	1979	
	JUNE	OCT./NOV.
For	27%	25%
Against	9	20
Don't Know Enough	54	40
No Opinion	10	15

The Gallup Poll: "Have you heard or read about SALT II, the proposed nuclear arms agreement between the U.S. and Russia? (If yes,) Everything considered, would you like to see the U.S. Senate ratify (vote in favor of) this proposed treaty, or not?"

	1979		
	MAR.	JUNE	SEPT.
Ratify (vote in favor of)	27%	34%	24%
Not	9	19	26
No Opinion	9	11	11
Haven't Heard Enough	55	36	39

Unfiltered Questions

The Roper Organization: "The U.S. and Russian negotiators have about reached agreement on a SALT Treaty, which would last until 1985 and limit each country to a maximum of 2,250 long-range nuclear missiles and bombers. As you know, there's a good deal of controversy about this treaty. Do you think the U.S. Senate should vote for this new SALT Treaty?"

	1978	1979				
	NOV.	JAN.	MAY	JULY	SEPT.	OCT.
For	42%	40%	33%	31%	30%	30%
Against	20	21	24	29	39	35
Mixed	17	19	20	21	15	19
Don't Know	21	20	23	19	17	17

Louis Harris Associates: "Do you favor or oppose the U.S. Senate ratifying the new SALT nuclear arms agreement between the U.S. and Russia?"

	1979
	SEPT.
Favor	42%
Oppose	37
Not Sure	21

Further divergence appears in two SALT II questions that were unfortunately asked only once during this period. Both were unfiltered questions, but unlike those in Tables 1 and 2 they were asked in "balanced alternative" format rather than agree-disagree format (see chapter 6). A May 1979 *Washington Post* survey asked respondents to choose between approving a treaty that would "leave the United States and Russia as equal as possible in military strength" or trying "to maintain military superiority over Russia." Support for the idea of a treaty (50 percent) in that context was chosen by only a margin of 8 percentage points over the military superiority option (42 percent). The Table 1 question on support for the idea of a treaty, it will be remembered, had produced support by at least a 3-to-1 margin during that time period.

A year earlier, in May 1978, Yankelovich's balanced alternative question produced the most lopsided margin of opposition to the treaty. This Yankelovich question asked respondents to choose between signing a weapons limitation agreement and thinking that "it is too risky." Here 56 percent of respondents chose the "too risky" option compared to only 32 percent who favored signing the Treaty. Simply introducing the element of risk in the wording of the question on the SALT issue seems to have made for a remarkable turn-around in the nature of public opinion.

The other basic divergence of opinion data in Tables 1 and 2 exists between the filtered and the unfiltered questions. In the NBC/AP poll in March 1979, the unfiltered question showed 71 percent support versus 18 percent opposition, while the filtered question showed 13 percent support versus 6 percent opposition. Similar results were found in the June 1979 CBS News/ *N. Y. Times* poll which recorded a 77-15 percent pro-con split for the unfiltered question and a 27-9 percent split for the filtered question.[10]

Overall, then, while the various surveys do converge on the conclusion that some general downward trend occurred in 1979, the exact point at which this decline started is not obvious.

This situation becomes important when one tries to pinpoint which of the many events in the spring and summer of 1979 caused the decline in support: the Senate SALT hearings, the testimony of Henry Kissinger at the hearings, the disclosures about Soviet troops in Cuba, the linkage of Soviet troop withdrawal to SALT passage by Senator Church, or the numerous other SALT comments expressed by political and military leaders and analysts. In terms of trends in declining support, the unfiltered questions show little convergence. The CBS News/*N.Y. Times* question showed lower support in the winter of 1978-79 than in June of 1979 when a similarly worded question was used. The Harris question shows support rising between January and April 1979 followed by a decline between April and May. A consistent decline is shown throughout 1979 by the NBC/AP general question and also for the Roper question on the Senate passage.

Of the three filtered questions, both the Gallup and CBS/*N.Y. Times* polls did register a significant decline between early summer and fall of 1979, but, as we noted, some disagreement occurs about when that decline began. Thus it becomes all but impossible to know which events led to the decline in public support.

Interpreting poll results from this period is further complicated because most polls did not ask for the reasons behind respondents' answers. In fact, only one poll (done by NBC/AP in February of 1979) asked respondents who favored the SALT II Treaty *why* they favored it. It is instructive to find that most people favored it for pocket-book reasons, i.e., because they saw it as a way to cut defense spending. Surprisingly, few respondents felt that the Treaty would improve relations with the U.S.S.R. or provide any other actively positive benefits. Thus declining support for the Treaty could have been anticipated; the public perceived that continued Soviet arms build-up precluded reductions in U.S. defense spending.

Other poll questions also hinted at some of the weak edges of support for the Treaty: Few members of the public felt that the U.S. was militarily stronger than the U.S.S.R.; only a small minority expressed great confidence in the

American negotiators of SALT II; and significant proportions of the public felt it was unlikely that the SALT II Treaty would reduce the risk of war with the Soviet Union. While it is plausible that this increase in skeptical or cautious attitudes undermined the public's support for the Treaty, none of the questions were repeated on subsequent polls. Therefore, it was impossible to investigate this hypothesis.

If data had been gathered from the same respondents across time, it would have been possible to see whose opinions shifted negatively during 1979 and which SALT-related news events affected public opinion. Did the rising opposition to the SALT II Treaty evolve mainly from the ranks of those who had previously been in the uncommitted or insufficient knowledge category? Did a hard core of supporters remain in favor of the Treaty throughout 1979, and how large was it? Without data collected from the same respondents across time it was not possible to answer these important policy questions.

The Panama Canal Treaty

The several polls conducted on the Panama Canal Treaty provide further evidence that the divergences found in the SALT II polls do not represent an isolated situation. Table 3 examines some trends in responses to polls conducted between the end of the summer of 1977 and early 1978, just before the Senate vote. During this period, the Carter administration was making strenuous efforts to win Senate (and public) approval.

As was found for SALT, there is some convergence of poll trends over this eight-month period. In the case of the Canal Treaty this showed increased support. The trends are indexed by subtracting the *pro* percentage from the usually larger *con* percentage for both 1977 and 1978 readings and recording the differences between 1977 polls and 1978 polls in the "Net Shift" column of Table 3. As in Tables 1 and 2,

Table 3 shows rather large differences in the pro-con distribution. For example, the May 1977 Opinion Research Center (ORC) question registered a 70 percentage point pro-con difference while the October 1977 Gallup question registered cons outnumbering pros by only a 10 percentage point difference.

Nonetheless, despite extreme spreads in the degree of public support, both polls converged in showing identical trends in the degree of net shift. In early 1978, ORC showed a 17 percentage point increase in public support, and Gallup showed 16 points more support. The Seasonwein poll verified a shift of about this magnitude (+11 points) over the same period.

The other three polls, however, indicate that virtually no shift had occurred. The California Poll question registered only a 4 percentage point increase over the same period. Moreover, the CBS/*Times* and the NBC polls both registered a trend in the *negative* direction, although of only 2 and 3 percentage points respectively. While the average of these six readings is about a 7 percentage point positive shift, there is a 20 percentage point spread between the high (+17 point) and low (–3 point) figures. That spread still is smaller than the difference of 35 percentage points found for the *same* period (i.e., the 72 percent con for ORC in February 1978 versus 37 percent con for Gallup in January of that year). The 35 point spread is attributable to question framing. But even a 20-point spread hardly represents a reliable trend in public opinion. It certainly would not be instructive to politicians wanting to trace changes in views of their constituents.

Table 4 summarizes the divisions of opinion on the Panama Canal Treaty as reported by polls between 1975 and 1978. Direct comparison across time is hampered because pollsters continually changed their questions.[11]

The CBS/*Times* question, like several others, introduced the information that the president of the United States had already signed the Treaty, information that could substantially affect a respondent's answer. Reference to "revised treaty" in several poll questions in early 1978 may have similarly influenced results. Use of the term "turn over" in many of the poll questions was perhaps even more unfortunate. While it did convey much of the political flavor of the public debate, it was not technically correct and reinforced existing public misperceptions and stereotypes that obscured other issues. Treaty questions that implicitly asked respondents about "giving away" the Panama Canal may have been less effective in measuring disapproval of the terms of the Treaty than in measuring concern over perceived loss of U.S. global dominance.

TABLE 3

REPEATED QUESTIONS ON THE PANAMA CANAL
(Between May 1977 and early 1978)

		May 1977	Feb. 1978	Net Shift
Opinion Research Corp.	Pro	8%	19%	
(Balanced alternative)	Con	78	72	
	Con-Pro	70	53	+17
		Oct. 1977	Jan. 1978	
The Gallup Poll	Pro	36%	43%	
(Favor-Oppose)	Con	46	37	
	Con-Pro	10	–6	+16
		Oct. 1977	Jan. 1978	
Seasonwein	Pro	28%	35%	
(Favor-Oppose)	Con	59	55	
	Con-Pro	31	20	+11
		Oct. 1977	Jan. 1978	
Field Research Corp. (California only)	Pro	35%	41%	
(Approve-Disapprove)	Con	44	46	
	Con-Pro	9	5	+4

		Oct. 1977	Jan. 1978	Net Shift
CBS News/ *N. Y. Times*				
	Pro	29%	29%	
(Approve-Disapprove)	Con	49	51	
	Con-Pro	20	22	−2

		Oct. 1977	Jan. 1978	
NBC News				
	Pro	30%	28%	
(Favor-Oppose)	Con	61	62	
	Con-Pro	31	34	−3

ORC: "Do you favor the United States continuing its ownership and control of the Panama Canal, or do you favor turning ownership and control of the Panama Canal over to the Republic of Panama?"

GALLUP: "Have you heard or read about the debate over the Panama Canal: The treaties would give Panama the Canal Zone by the year 2000, but the United States would retain the right to defend the Canal against a third nation. Do you favor or oppose these treaties between the U.S. and Panama?"

SEASONWEIN: "The Senate is now considering a new Panama Canal Treaty that President Carter has submitted to it. The Treaty calls for Panama to become the owner of the Canal in the year 2000. Are you inclined to favor or oppose this Treaty?"

FIELD RESEARCH: "(As you may have heard) the Panama Canal treaties call for the gradual transfer of control over the Canal to the country of Panama by the year 2000 with the U.S. retaining military defense rights. From what you have seen or heard, do you personally approve or disapprove of these treaties?"

CBS/ *Times*: "The Senate now has to debate the treaties that President Carter signed granting control of the Panama Canal to the Republic of Panama in the year 2000. Do you approve or disapprove of those treaties?"

NBC: "The new treaty between the United States and Panama calls for the United States to turn over ownership of the Canal to Panama at the end of this century. However, this treaty still has to be approved by the Senate. Do you favor or oppose approval of this treaty by the Senate?"

Informational survey questions indicated that most people had not thought much about the Canal until the Treaty negotiations were almost concluded. A 1975 National Opinion Research Corporation study found only about a third of the public understood the basic terms of the 1904 Treaty under which Panama ceded the Canal Zone to the United States. In January 1978, a Gallup survey found that only 8 percent (up from 4 percent in 1977) of the public

TABLE 4

APPROVAL-DISAPPROVAL FIGURES ON PANAMA CANAL TREATY
(FIRST FIGURE: PERCENTAGE IN FAVOR/SECOND FIGURE: PERCENTAGE OPPOSED)

	OPINION RE-SEARCH	HARRIS	GALLUP	CBS/N.Y. TIMES	NBC/AP	ROPER	YANKEL-OVICH	CADDELL
1975 June	12-66* (29-48)							
1976	13-75*			24-52 (May)				
1977 January						24-53		
February								
March							29-53	
April								
May	8-78*							27-51
June/July								
August								
September		26-51	36-46*	29-49*	30-61*			
October								30-55
1978 January			43-37*	29-51*	28-62*			
February	19-72*	31-40*						
March		29-60						
(Vote 1 Ratifica-tion Mar. 16) April		37-44						
(Vote 2 Ratifica-tion Apr. 18) May								
June		35-49				30-52		
July/August								
September					34-56			
October					45-47			

*Same question repeated

understood the major relevant aspects of the Treaty. Cross-tabular analysis revealed that the respondents least familiar with the Treaty negotiations were the ones most opposed to the Treaty, indicating the need once again to distinguish informed and uninformed opinion.

Questions on U.S.-Soviet Relations

Many of the same divergences appear in the portrayals of public opinion on general East-West relations during the 1970s. During the Vietnam war years of the late 1960s and early 1970s, U.S.-Soviet relations lost much of the harshness and shrillness that characterized the intensive cold war of the 1950s and early 1960s. Public opinion toward the Soviet Union grew more positive during the period of detente in the mid-1970s. But a cold war atmosphere returned with the concern over the Soviet arms buildup, Soviet activity in Africa, and the Carter administration's attacks on U.S.S.R. human rights violations. Unfortunately, few questions on U.S.-U.S.S.R. relations were repeated after mid-1978, providing little chance to gauge the effect of the Soviet incursion into Afghanistan and the reported Soviet arms buildup. Poll data that may be used to analyze public opinion trends concerning U.S.-Soviet relations are arrayed in Tables 5, 6, and 7. Table 5 deals with the general tenor of relations, Table 6 more specifically with the issue of detente, and Table 7 with the issue of human rights.

The first Roper question in Table 5 shows that between 1974 and 1977 an increased proportion of the public (from 33 to 42 percent) expressed the view that we should make a "major effort" to improve relations with the Soviet Union; this trend is substantiated by a corresponding proportional decline noted in the "no effort"category. The second Roper question also indicates a positive direction of trend between 1974 and 1977, but at a far less significant rate of 3 percentage points—a 36 percent "strengthen ties" response in 1977 versus a 33 percent "strengthen ties" response in

1974. Moreover, the second question shows no movement after 1975, while the first question indicates a growing desire for improved relations in each year between 1974 and 1977.[12]

TABLE 5

POLL QUESTIONS AND TRENDS ON U.S.-SOVIET RELATIONS

The Roper Organization:	"There are many problems facing our nation today.... How much effort should the government make in...trying to improve relations between the United States and Russia?"

	JUNE 1974	JUNE 1975	JUNE 1976	JUNE 1977	JUNE 1978
Major effort	33%	38%	37%	42%	42%
Some effort	43	44	45	43	40
No effort	18	13	13	18	13
Don't know	6	6	6	5	5

The Roper Organization:	"The United States has formed ties of varying degrees with different nations in the world. Here is a list of countries. Tell me for ... Russia, what would be best for us in the long run: strengthen our ties with them, continue things about as they are, or lessen our commitments to them?"

	JAN. 1974	JAN. 1975	1976	JAN. 1977
Strengthen ties	33%	36%	NA*	36%
Continue as is	30	31	NA	28
Lessen commitments	25	22	NA	22
Don't know	12	11	NA	14

The Harris Survey:	"Do you think relations between the U.S. and Russia will get better, worse, or stay about the same?"

	SEPT. 1970	MAY 1972	JUNE† 1973	1974	1975	OCT.** 1976	1977
Get better	28%	28%	66%	NA	NA	31%	NA
Stay the same	57	57	24	NA	NA	38	NA
Get worse	7	10	2	NA	NA	14	NA
Don't know	8	5	8	NA	NA	7	NA

| Potomac Associates: | "Do you think relations between the United States and the Soviet Union will get better, get worse or stay about the same?" | | | |

	MAY 1974	1975	MAY 1976	1977
Get better	27%	NA	23%	NA
Stay the same	50	NA	49	NA
Get worse	10	NA	19	NA
Don't know	13	NA	9	NA

*Not asked
†Preamble to 1973 question: "Compared to five years ago, . . ."
**Asked by Potomac Associates

However, the general theme of "improvement" suggested by the responses to the Roper questions runs counter to the results of the next two questions, which deal with how well U.S.-U.S.S.R. relations were in fact progressing. At roughly the same time that Roper was receiving positive public response on easing U.S.-Soviet relations, Harris questions reported a drop in those who felt that U.S.-Soviet relations would improve (from 60 percent in 1973 to 31 percent in 1976). Potomac Associates also detected a negative trend on expected future relations with the Soviet Union between 1974 and 1976: a 4 percentage point decrease in the proportion who felt that these relations were getting better and a 9 percentage point increase of those who felt that they were getting worse. Thus, during the same period that the public seemed more open and optimistic about improved U.S.-Soviet relations, they were becoming more pessimistic about how these relations were actually developing.[13]

The same contrasting pattern of responses appears in Table 6, which examines the topic of detente. While the public continued to approve the general policy of detente, only a handful of people felt that the U.S. was gaining anything from it. The pattern is found for both sets of questions asked about each topic.

Despite these generally reassuring degrees of consistency in Table 6, however, there are several important differences and divergences. The unfiltered Harris question indicates up to a 7-to-1 margin of support across that time period, but the Caddell question never exceeded a 4-to-1 margin. While the Caddell question shows no greater support of detente between 1975 and 1977, the Harris questions show a 10 percentage point increase in support. While the Roper question shows increased feeling that the Soviets had gained more than the U.S. from detente between 1975 and 1977, the Yankelovich question shows little such trend. Perhaps the most disturbing finding, however, occurs for a general

TABLE 6

POLL QUESTIONS AND TRENDS ON DETENTE

A. Principle of Detente

Harris: "Do you favor or oppose detente, that is the United States and Russia seeking out areas of agreement and cooperation?"

	DEC. 1975	MAR. 1976	AUG. 1976	MAR. 1977	APR.-MAY 1978	JUNE 1978
Favor	62%	59%	73%	75%	71%	69%
Oppose	15	23	16	10	16	19
Not sure	23	18	11	15	14	22

Caddell: "Do you favor or oppose moves toward detente?" (Asked only of those who had heard of detente):

	JAN. 1975	MAR. 1976	JUNE 1977
Favor	38%	30%	41%
Oppose	9	19	13
Not sure	10	15	22
Don't know (detente)	43	35	25

CBS/*New York Times:* "What do you think the United States should do—should the United States try harder to relax tensions with the Russians or instead should the United States get tougher in its dealings with the Russians?"

	JUNE 1978
Relax	30%
Tougher	53
Both	6
No opinion	11

B. Who Benefits?

Roper: "Has detente been of more benefit to the United States, Russia, or both about equally?"

	JAN. 1975	MAR. 1976	JUNE 1977
More advantage to U.S.	3%	3%	3%
Advantage to both equally	36	33	30
More advantage to Russians	31	42	37
Don't Know	31	22	31

Yankelovich, Skelly & White:

"How do you feel about our relations with Russia—who do you feel benefits the most from our closer, more cooperative relations with the Soviets, which are sometimes called detente?"

	AUG. 1975	1976	APR. 1977
Mostly the U.S.	3%	NA	5%
Both countries equally	19	NA	26
Mostly the Soviet Union	45	NA	46
Neither one, not sure	33	NA	23

question in which the word "detente" did not appear. At the same time that Harris's June 1978 poll was showing 3.5-to-1 *support* for detente, a June 1978 CBS/*N.Y. Times* poll showed a 2-to-1 preference for "getting tougher with the Russians" rather than "trying harder to relax tensions." Either the term *detente* had a more positive connotation than "relaxation of tension," or perhaps in comparison with the "get tough" option in the CBS/*N.Y. Times* question, detente seemed far less attractive. In this latter connection, the distinction is similar to one noted earlier about introducing the element of risk in relations with the Soviet Union in connection with SALT II.

Finally, Table 7 briefly examines 1977 poll data on the U.S.-Soviet issue of human rights, an important element of Carter administration policy of the time. While no trend data are presented for these questions, there is a surprising convergence of poll support for the policy, despite the extremely diverse set of questions employed. Support across the first four questions in Table 7 varied only 2 percent, from 53 to 55 percent. Opposition varied only 10 percent, from 21 to 31 percent. Harris found 53 percent rating Carter's job as good or excellent on standing up for Russian dissidents and Public Interest Research found approval of Carter's stance by the same percentage. Yankelovich reported 55 percent favoring Carter's continuing to speak out even if it meant more difficulties in the SALT talks, and Roper found 54 percent approving Carter's championship of human rights in all other countries.

TABLE 7

POLL QUESTIONS AND TRENDS ON HUMAN RIGHTS

Roper: "President Carter has been publicly critical of the nations that deny human rights to their citizens. Some people approve of Carter's stand on human rights on the grounds that the United States must champion human rights throughout the world. Others disapprove on the grounds that it is interference with the affairs of other nations and worsens our relations with these countries. How do you feel? Do you approve or disapprove Carter's championing of human rights in other countries?"

	APPROVE	DISAPPROVE	DON'T KNOW
May 1977	54%	31%	15%

Public Interest
Opinion Research: "Would you favor President Carter continuing to speak out on human rights in Russia and elsewhere even if that makes it harder to reach arms control limits with the Soviet Union?"

	FAVOR	OPPOSE	UNDECIDED
June 1977	53%	29%	18%

Harris: "Would you rate the job President Carter has done on his standing up for the rights of the Soviet dissidents as excellent, good, only fair or poor?"

	EXCELLENT, GOOD	FAIR, POOR	NOT SURE
April 1977	53%	21%	26%
July 1977*	52	28	20

Yankelovich: "Do you personally feel that President Carter should or should not continue to complain to the Russians about the suppression of human rights, even if it slows down detente and the chance for an arms agreement?"

	SHOULD	SHOULD NOT	NO OPINION
March 1977	55%	26%	19%

CBS: "President Carter has recently critized the Soviet government for denying the rights of some of its own citizens. Do you approve or disapprove of the president telling the Soviet government how to treat their own citizens; or can't you really say?

	APPROVE	DIS-APPROVE	CAN'T SAY	NO ANSWER
April 1977	26%	38%	32%	4%

*July wording: "How would you rate the job President Carter has done on his statements condemning the lack of human rights in Russia for those who criticize their system?"

On the face of it, the great variations in wording and phrasing used in these four questions seem no greater than those introduced by the fifth question in Table 7, the one used by the CBS/*Times* poll. But in marked contrast to the first four questions, the CBS/*Times* question actually shows more disapproval (38 percent) of Carter's human rights stand than approval (26 percent). Perhaps the crucial question phrasing is the CBS/*Times*'s introduction of the concept of "telling" another government how to run its country. The concept of interference in the internal affairs of another country, our survey results in the next chapter suggest, violates a basic American tenet of appropriate foreign policy.

In summary, the same disturbing lack of convergences found in SALT II poll findings is found for poll results on other aspects of U.S.-Soviet relations. Like the Panama Canal polls, different questions asked by different poll organizations occasionally may produce similar conclusions when the concepts involved are similar. Considerable public support was evident for the abstract principles of detente and arms limitation and, to a lesser extent, for promoting human rights; these feelings are offset by the expectation that eventually the Soviets will get the best of any agreements we make with them. While the polls portray the public as more optimistic than pessimistic on relations with the Soviet Union, no consensus was evident about whether the public saw the gap in U.S.-U.S.S.R. relations widening or narrowing. Questions that characterized criticism of human rights violations as "telling" other countries how to run their internal affairs, that identified "the beneficiary" from detente, or that appealed to public sentiments about "getting tough with the Russians" contributed significantly to the problem of analyzing trends.

The United Nations

We conclude this chapter on a more optimistic note, an example of clear poll convergence. The debate over United States participation in the United Nations is a long-range policy issue on which more than thirty years of data are available. We will examine three questions that were asked repeatedly from 1965 to 1977. The first question, asked by the National Opinion Research Corporation (NORC), required the respondent to make a clear-cut pro-con stand.

"Do you think our government should continue to belong to the United Nations or should we pull out of it now?"

The second question, included in polls conducted by Potomac Associates during the 1970s, asked respondents to agree or disagree with this statement:

"The United States should cooperate fully with the U.N."

The third one requiring an evaluative response, was asked by Gallup:

"In general, do you feel the U.N. is doing a good job in trying to solve the problems it has to face?"

The three questions thus assess different types of public support for the United Nations. In separate surveys in 1975, we find that 51 percent of the respondents said the U.N. had been doing a poor job, while Potomac Associates showed only 30 percent in disagreement with the statement that the U.S. should cooperate fully with the U.N.; the 1975 NORC General Social Survey found only 18 percent saying we should pull out of the U.N. These data suggest, therefore, that the three questions are well ordered. People are more willing to say that the U.N. is doing a poor job than to say we should not cooperate fully with the U.N. or, in turn, to say we should pull out of the U.N. This characterization is supported by a 1977 Roper survey in which all three questions were asked: While the overall levels of support had generally increased, the general trend remained about the same—39 percent "poor job," 30 percent "should not cooperate fully," and 13 percent "pull out."

Figure 1 shows that the three questions generated consistent trend patterns for studies conducted between 1967 and 1977. Figure 1 has been constructed to portray "net" differences in opinion by subtracting the proportions of the public giving negative U.N. responses from the proportion giving positive responses. What is most remarkable, given the previous data in this chapter, is that the three trend lines more or less move up and down in unison. Support for the U.N. can be seen to decline between the mid-1960s and 1972, rise slightly between 1972 and 1973, decline between 1974 and 1976, and rebound again from 1976 until 1977.

Summary

This chapter has offered a litany of divergences in poll data on four major issues. Some of these divergences seem to be the result of differences in question formats used by the multiplicity of polling organizations. Some arose because pollsters chose to examine different aspects of a given issue. Others can be attributed to the fact that one or more

FIGURE 1:

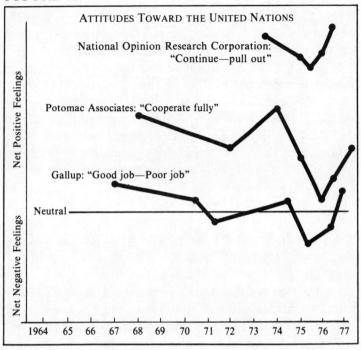

ATTITUDES TOWARD THE UNITED NATIONS

National Opinion Research Corporation:
"Continue—pull out"

Potomac Associates: "Cooperate fully"

Gallup: "Good job—Poor job"

Neutral

Net Positive Feelings

Net Negative Feelings

1964 65 66 67 68 69 70 71 72 73 74 75 76 77

significant questions contained a single emotion-laden word that seemed to skew poll results sharply in one direction or another.

What conclusions can we draw from these observations? It would be a mistake to try to reduce divergences by curtailing the diversity of the polling industry. Each issue needs to be examined from a variety of perspectives. The current plethora of poll findings from a broad range of independent polling agencies helps assure that major public opinion issues get close scrutiny. Yet it is precisely because of this freedom of choice that polls provide divergent results. What we need, then, are effective methods of communicating the significance of these differences to poll users and to pollsters themselves.

At a minimum, we need to know how, why, and under what circumstances the findings were obtained. Poll findings should be accompanied by a statement about what aspects of an issue the poll sought to examine and why this aspect was chosen over others. Ideally, such a statement should also list other polling agencies that had studied the issue and a summary of what their findings were.

Given the way polls are conducted and financed, it seems unrealistic to expect pollsters to provide all of this information. We submit, however, that it is a proper goal for the profession, and we are encouraged that the public disclosure code of the National Council on Public Polls goes a long way toward attaining this goal. The code requires that members of the Council provide with the release of their findings of all public polls eight types of information about how the findings were obtained. These include disclosure of poll sponsorship, sample size, and the complete wording of questions. Only by further research and by acceptance by all pollsters of the principles of the Council's code can the profession continue to raise its standards for poll reporting.

Notes

1. Entire issues of *Sociological Methods and Research* (#6, 1977) and the *Journal of Marketing Research* (#14, 1977) were devoted to methodological issues in polling and survey research.

2. Bernard Roshco, "Polling on Panama—Si; Don't Know; Hell, No!" *Public Opinion Quarterly*, Winter 1978, pp. 551-562.

3. Elizabeth Perkins and John Robinson, "The Public Looks at the United Nations: Implications for Foreign Policy" (Paper presented at the Third Annual Conference of the Midwest Association of Public Opinion Research, Chicago, IL). The results are also available through the 27 July 1977 statement to the Senate Foreign Relations Committee by the League of Women Voters Education Fund.

4. Martin Lipset, "The Wavering Polls," *The Public Interest* 43(1976): 79-80.

5. Seymour M. Lipset and William Schneider, "Polls for the White House and the Rest of Us," *Encounter,* November 1977, p. 26.

6. Howard Schuman and Stanley Presser, "Public Opinion and Public Ignorance: The Fine Line Between Attitudes and Non-Attitudes," *American Journal of Sociology* 85(1980): 1214-1225.

7. William J. Lanouette, "Polls and Pols" in *Polling on the Issues,* Albert H. Cantril, ed. (Cabin John, MD: Seven Locks Press, 1980), pp. 100-101.

8. The three sets of questions do appear to produce the following convergences across the one year period from mid-year 1978 to mid-year 1979: 67-22 (June 1978) to 68-22 (April 1979) for NBC/AP; 72-17 (June 1978) to 72-18 (May 1979) for ABC/Harris, and 78-14 (June 1978) to 77-15 (June 1979) for CBS/*N.Y. Times*. These convergences suggest that support had increased in late 1978 and early 1979, but that support had settled back to that mid-1978 level by mid-1979. Nonetheless, there is considerable divergence across the three polling organizations concerning the magnitude of increased support and the time when support for the Treaty had peaked in 1979. NBC/AP, for example, shows a 14 point increase and a 16 point decline, while Harris/ABC shows only a 3 point increase and a 3 point decline, while the questions used by CBS/*N.Y. Times* varied too much in the 1978-79 period to detect any trends.

9. A Harris survey conducted in September of 1979 showed virtually no difference from a May 1979 survey in public acceptance of two of the three reasons for supporting some arms limitation treaty and only a 13 percent decline was reported for the third. Yet, on the Harris press release of the firm's September results, major emphasis was put on the slim 42-37 percent edge for Senate passage of the SALT Treaty shown in Table 2. These figures were contrasted with the May 1979 pro-con balance of 72-18 percent in favor of the idea of a new agreement, with the conclusion that "public support for SALT II has taken a tumble." This conclusion was reached despite the fact that the May 1979 question was not repeated in September and the September question had not been asked earlier.

10. A cross-tabular analysis of the true CBS/*Times* questions in the June 1979 survey produced the following interesting dissection of where the divergence in results occurs.

	Favor	Oppose	DK/NA		
Vote for	26%	1%	0%	=	27%
Vote against	5	4	0	=	9%
DK enough	46	10	8	=	64%
	77%	15%	8%	=	100%

The greatest consistency is produced in the first row of the table where almost all (26 percent out of 27 percent) of those who favor Senate passage also favor the idea of an agreement. The second row of the table shows that there is almost an even split of support for the idea of a treaty among those who would favor Senate approval; this is consistent with a model that sees opposition to the Treaty as coming from two sources—general opposition to the idea of a treaty and specific opposition to the terms of the SALT II Treaty. The final row in the table also produces an interesting result: Those who felt they didn't know enough to have an opinion on Senate passage split about 5-to-1 in favor of the idea of an agreement, very similar to the 6-to-1 support among those who did feel they knew enough.

11. Opposition to the Treaty still continued after its passage in April 1978. Military protection arrangements included in the approved draft apparently did not allay public perceptions that relinquishing control would increase U.S. vulnerability. Possibly the final provisions of the Treaty were not effectively conveyed to the public. According to State Department analyst Bernard Roshco:

> When it was all over, the basic finding of approximately five-to-three opposed, which had emerged when the issue of the treaties became salient, seemed to have re-emerged. The trend that was confirmed most strongly could have been graphed with a straight horizontal line. (Roshco, "Polling on Panama," p. 562).

12. However, between 1974 and 1977 the perception that the U.S. should strengthen rather than loosen ties increased for practically *all* countries about

which Roper inquired—not only the Soviet Union, but France, Japan, and South American countries. Since the increase was lower for the Soviet Union than for other countries, it may contradict the trend in the "effort" question.

13. It is, of course, possible to offer post hoc explanations of why the two sets of questions invited different responses. In periods of worsening relations, people may see the need to make a major effort to "improve relations" or to "strengthen ties." This was the explanation that State Department analysts arrived at to explain these differences.

5 The Ten-City Study

IN 1976 AND 1977, world affairs councils and other groups in ten American cities sponsored a series of "town meetings." Their purpose was to give officials of the State Department firsthand exposure to public reactions to U.S. foreign policies and to provide additional opportunities for public expression on these policies. Before each of the meetings, approximately 300 people over age eighteen, chosen at random in their communities, were interviewed by telephone. The intention was to allow a wider representation of public opinion in each community than could be given by the relatively few who would be heard at the meetings. Most of the fifteen-to-twenty-minute telephone interviews were conducted using a variant of the random digit dial method of locating respondents.[1] The list of the cities[2] involved and the survey fieldwork organizations conducting the interviews along with other pertinent survey details are listed in Table 8.

The questionnaires varied across the ten cities, but there were several common elements. As shown in the prototype in Appendix A, each began with some simple and general orientation questions about feelings of isolationism and alienation and the importance of goals and values in U.S. foreign policy. The subsequent questions then focused on particular policy areas. They varied, depending on the topic discussed at the town meeting in each city. They included a series of five to ten questions on foreign aid, five to seven questions on East-West relations, three to six questions on human rights, two to five items on foreign trade and business, and two to four items on arms sales or interventionist activities.

TABLE 8

THE TEN-CITY STUDY

CITY	DATE	INTERVIEWING ORGANIZATIONS	SAMPLE SIZE
Pittsburgh	January 1976	Guide-Post Research, Noble Interviewing	299†
San Francisco	March 1976	The Field Institute	309
Portland, Oregon	March 1976	The Field Institute	306
Milwaukee	April 1976	University of Wisconsin-Milwaukee	292
Minnesota*	April 1976	Custom Research	300
Los Angeles	May 1977	Facts Consolidated	300†
St. Louis	September 1977	Marie Winters Interviewing	315†
Portland, Oregon	September 1977	Dianne Henson Interviewing	302†
Cleveland	October 1977	Marketing Research of Cleveland	301†
Pittsburgh	November 1977	Guide-Post Research	200
Atlanta	December 1977	Marilyn F. Jackson & Associates	301†

*Statewide sample
†Sample chosen by variant of random digit dial method by Communication Research Center of Cleveland State University.

Finally, personal background information was collected on the respondents' sex, age, and education (and in some cities, income or political party affiliation).

Differences in Overall Responses

Tables 9-12, giving highlights of responses by city, are arranged by general topics: Table 9 dealing with East-West relations; Table 10 with Third World questions; Table 11 with human rights; Table 12 with isolationism and generally related matters; and Table 13 with the general value questions that began the surveys. Only one paraphrased response for each question is presented in order to allow the reader a simple overview and comparison of results. A detailed analysis of these data has already been published (Robinson and Holm, 1977; Kettering Foundation, 1978). Because the potential for ambiguity in drawing any generalizations about national opinion from a study of ten preselected cities is considerable, we have not attempted to summarize the state of public opinion at the time from a single question or a single number.

Nonetheless, the reader will note enough broad convergences in responses across the ten cities to warrant some general conclusions about the nature of foreign policy thinking in the early post-Vietnam era. These impressions are strengthened when we compare our results to those obtained in national surveys conducted at about the same time by *different researchers* asking *different questions* in *different formats*. Such convergences in poll data are hardly an inevitable occurrence, as examples cited earlier attest. The readers should consult Appendix A for the exact wording of each question. They have only been paraphrased and reduced to single numbers in Tables 9-13.

Responses by Topics

East-West Relations: Table 9 reveals that even before the disagreements between the U.S. and U.S.S.R. over Africa, human rights, and arms talks, considerable uneasiness about our relations with the Soviet Union was evident; much of this public apprehensiveness probably can be traced to the days of the cold war. As reflected in Table 9, almost three times as many people agreed with the statement that "the United States cannot trust the Russians to live up to their agreements" as disagreed. Almost half felt we should keep militarily well ahead of the U.S.S.R.; yet less

TABLE 9

OPINIONS ON EAST-WEST RELATIONS
(Exact question wording shown in Appendix A)

Position	1976						1977					
CITY MONTH SAMPLE SIZE (N =)	PITT. FEB. (299)	S. FR. MAR. (309)	PORT. MAR. (306)	MILW. APR. (292)	MINN. APR. (300)	TOTAL	L.A. MAY (300)	ST. L. SEPT. (315)	PORT. SEPT. (302)	CLEV. OCT. (301)	ATL. DEC. (301)	TOTAL
Percentage Indicating Acceptance												
U.S.-Soviet relations improving	NA†	38%	35%	27%	32%	27%	NA	NA	NA	NA	NA	NA
U.S. cannot trust Russia	66	47	58	62	61	59	57	66	60	60	61	61
U.S. should keep well ahead of Russia	51*	30	39	46	42	41	47	48	38	49	52	47
U.S. is well ahead of Russia	NA	NA	NA	NA	NA	NA	12	18	18	19	20	18
U.S. should spend more on military	NA	NA	NA	NA	NA	NA	30	25	NA	26	40	29
Favor U.S.-Soviet trade	22	20	25	24	27	24	NA	NA	22	NA	NA	NA
Extend credit to Soviets	60	75	70	65	66	67	NA	NA	72	NA	NA	NA
Oppose using Soviet trade politically	14*	24	27	17*	27	22	NA	NA	NA	NA	NA	NA
Criticize Russia on human rights	44	53	52	41	41	46	43	51	41	51	45	46
Russia benefitted more from detente	47	46	44	32	41	42	NA	NA	24	NA	NA	NA
U.S.-Soviet improvement a good thing	NA	NA	NA	NA	NA	NA	69	78	NA	72	71	73
Soviet-Chinese relations good	NA	NA	NA	NA	NA	NA	9	8	NA	10	NA	9
Improve relations with China over Russia	NA	NA	NA	NA	NA	NA	8	8	13	7	NA	9
Improve with Russia over China	NA	NA	NA	NA	NA	NA	6	5	4	4	NA	5
SALT over human rights or Soviet trade	NA	NA	NA	NA	NA	NA	71	71	NA	72	68	70

*Slightly different wording
†NA—Question not asked

than one in five felt we were well ahead. Nearly half of the respondents in the 1976 surveys felt the U.S.S.R. had gained more from detente than the United States. (Less than 3 percent felt the U.S. had gained more; the rest said both had benefited or had no opinion.) In addition, almost two-thirds polled in all ten cities (see Table 13) felt that stopping the spread of communism was a very important goal of U.S. foreign policy, positioning it among the top five goals of foreign policy.

At the same time, several signs of a more conciliatory orientation were present. Six times as many people interviewed in the 1977 surveys felt detente had been a good thing rather than a bad thing. Trade with the Soviets was favored by an almost 2-to-1 margin in the 1976 surveys,[3] and most of those in favor opposed the idea of attaching political strings to that trade. Three times as many people felt U.S.-U.S.S.R. relations were getting better rather than getting worse, although most people felt little had changed. Deep interest in nuclear arms agreements with the Soviet Union was evident from both the 75 percent who saw it as a very important goal of U.S. policy (Table 13) and from a percentage almost that large who assigned it a higher priority than human rights or trade with the U.S.S.R.

The public was almost evenly divided on whether or not to criticize the Soviet Union for its human rights violations. Fewer than one in ten would criticize the Soviet Union for its lack of basic democratic institutions, however.

Finally, the public did not favor exploiting conflicts between the Soviet Union and China. While fewer than 10 percent perceived the relations between these two countries as good, fewer than 15 percent favored improving relations with one country over the other. Among those with a preference, slightly more people favored better relations with China than with the Soviet Union.

Third World: The United States encountered unprecedented difficulties in dealing with the Third World in the

1970s. Certain less-developed countries had criticized our involvement in Vietnam, had openly confronted us in the United Nations, and had also steeply raised the prices of their raw materials and goods, notably oil and coffee. In view of these price increases, it was instructive to find that few people in our surveys were willing to accept the idea that the U.S. had generally exploited Third World countries economically by paying low prices for their commodities and raw materials.

Despite these developments and the perceived lack of clear successes in our foreign aid programs in the past, the public, as portrayed in Table 10, still favored the principle of foreign aid by more than a 2-to-1 margin; they also expressed a willingness to help personally in that effort in the 1976 polls. Moreover, the goal of fighting world hunger was rated near the top of foreign policy goals for the country (see Table 13), with two out of every three people interviewed in the 1977 surveys feeling that the U.S. had a moral responsibility to help the less fortunate of the world; an even larger proportion felt foreign aid was justified to help these countries develop their own resources. Moreover, few people appeared willing to accept as valid reasons for denying aid the arguments that foreign aid hurts the U.S. economy or that the Third World could develop on its own.

However, considerable public discontent was evident on the matter of *how* aid was to be distributed. In the 1977 polls, the perceptions that aid benefited the wrong people or had been wasted by the receiving countries were accepted as sound reasons for discontinuing aid; this was even true for most people who favored aid. In the 1976 survey, almost twice as many people expressed a willingness to contribute aid directly rather than to have their taxes raised for that purpose. Apparently Americans felt that aid would be used more effectively if given directly and channeled privately rather than through a government agency.

More support was evident for the principle of directing aid to those in greatest need. As Table 13 shows, consider-

TABLE 10

OPINIONS ON THIRD WORLD AND AID
(Exact question wording shown in Appendix A)

CITY MONTH SAMPLE SIZE (N =)	1976						1977					
	PITT. FEB. (299)	S. FR. MAR. (309)	PORT. MAR. (306)	MILW. APR. (292)	MINN. APR. (300)	TOTAL	L.A. MAY (300)	ST. L. SEPT. (315)	PORT. SEPT. (302)	CLEV. OCT. (301)	ATL. DEC. (301)	TOTAL
Position						*Percentage Indicating Acceptance*						
U.S. should help less-developed countries (*LDCs*)	55%	67%	47%	59%	57%	57%	52%	64%	NA†	58%	56%	58%
Would pay more taxes to prevent starvation	29	34	23	25	40	30	NA	NA	NA	NA	NA	NA
Would contribute money to prevent starvation	54	58	48	61	47	53	NA	NA	NA	NA	NA	NA
Would reduce living standard to prevent starvation	18	36	28	25	33	28	NA	NA	NA	NA	NA	NA
Would do one of the above three	58	71	73	64	74	66	NA	NA	NA	NA	NA	NA
U.S. exploits poor countries on raw materials	18*	48	34	29	31	33	NA	NA	NA	15	12	13
Aid only to countries that do what we want	44	37	38	52	47	44	NA	NA	41	NA	NA	NA
Arguments *for* aid:												
Stop communism	NA	NA	NA	NA	NA	NA	42	49	NA	43	46	45
Develop independence	NA	NA	NA	NA	NA	NA	69	73	NA	72	69	71
Avoid revolution	NA	NA	NA	NA	NA	NA	35	42	NA	38	39	39
Our moral responsibility	NA	NA	NA	NA	NA	NA	64	65	NA	63	61	63
Arguments *against* aid:												
Wrong people get aid	NA	NA	NA	NA	NA	NA	63	63	NA	71	63	65

TABLE 11

	Aid wasted	Hurts economy	Any country develops
PITT. FEB. (299)	NA	NA	NA
S. FR. MAR. (309)	NA	NA	NA
PORT. MAR. (306)	NA	NA	NA
MILW. APR. (292)	NA	NA	NA
MINN. APR. (300)	NA	NA	NA
TOTAL	NA	NA	NA
L.A. MAY (300)	56	39	NA
ST. L. SEPT. (315)	61	39	21
PORT. SEPT. (302)	NA	NA	NA
CLEV. OCT. (301)	64	38	28
ATL. DEC. (301)	65	37	28
TOTAL	62	38	25

*Slightly different wording
†NA—Question not asked

OPINIONS ON HUMAN RIGHTS AND DICTATORSHIPS
(Exact question wording shown in Appendix A)

| | 1976 | | | | | | 1977 | | | | | |
CITY MONTH SAMPLE SIZE (N =)	PITT. FEB. (299)	S. FR. MAR. (309)	PORT. MAR. (306)	MILW. APR. (292)	MINN. APR. (300)	TOTAL	L.A. MAY (300)	ST. L. SEPT. (315)	PORT. SEPT. (302)	CLEV. OCT. (301)	ATL. DEC. (301)	TOTAL
Position												
				Percentage Indicating Acceptance								
Aid only to democracies	35%	25%	32%	39%	33%	33%	NA†	NA	32%	NA	NA	NA
Alliance only to democracies	25	24	29	29	31	28	NA	NA	NA	NA	NA	NA
U.S. should criticize human rights violators	NA	NA	NA	NA	NA	NA	34*	51	43	52	46	48
Human rights over SALT or Soviet trade	NA	NA	NA	NA	NA	NA	16	18	NA	12	17	16
Refuse business with rights violators	NA	NA	NA	NA	NA	NA	47*	66	NA	68	61	65

*Slightly different wording
†NA—Question not asked

ably more support was found for stopping world hunger than for the principle of aid in general. A more direct question (asked only in the 1976 Pittsburgh study and its 1977 replication) found less than half as much support for the policy of "triage"—that is for aid to those most likely to attain self-sufficiency eventually—than for aid to those in greatest immediate need. In the Pittsburgh surveys, respondents were also asked what we should expect in return for our foreign aid. The majority spontaneously replied "nothing," and it can be seen in Table 10 that less than half of those interviewed in the 1976 surveys agreed with the statement that the U.S. should help only those countries "that will help us do the things we want to do in the world." In their responses to questions both about aid to the neediest and on what we should expect in return, the strong sense of idealism and humanitarianism about aid was clearly evident.

Human Rights: While a few questions touching on democracies and dictatorships were included in the 1976 surveys, only the 1977 surveys actually used the term "human rights." This had become a key element in the Carter administration's foreign policy, but Table 11 indicates at the time of the surveys the public was fairly evenly divided on the human rights issue. However, more people in our surveys felt the U.S. should criticize human rights violations than felt it was not our country's business. Virtually the same division of opinion was found when the same question was asked with specific regard to the Soviet Union, indicating no consciously greater application of this principle to our major adversary.

The data in Table 11 also indicate that in contrast to the half of those surveyed who would criticize the Soviet Union for its violations of human rights, only one in six considered it a more important goal than SALT talks or trade with the Soviet Union. This was true, even though responses to open-ended questions in our 1977 surveys (not shown) indicated that the Soviet Union was the country spontaneously nominated as the major world violator of human rights. Much the same impression emerged from a 1976 question (Table 9) in which few people wanted any such political strings attached to our trade with the Soviets; and only minorities agreed with the statement that we should restrict our foreign aid or alliances to those countries with a democratic form of government.

Nonetheless, one question did suggest more solid support for emphasis on human rights in foreign policy. Almost two-thirds of those interviewed agreed with the statement that the U.S. should refuse to do business with countries that violated human rights. Notably, the question was not entirely phrased in the abstract nor without raising the issue of cost; it closed with the proviso: "even if the U.S. loses a lot of business doing it." Questions that reminded respondents that trade restrictions hit their own pocketbooks rather than the economy in general might have produced a different result.

Any convergences on human rights policy would be remarkable given the widely different interpretations people place on the term "human rights." When we asked respondents in the 1977 surveys to describe what human rights meant to them, a wide variety of responses was recorded. The most common response was "freedom of speech." The second most common was "freedom of religion," not, we should note, "freedom of political choice." For others, the term suggested freedom of mobility, freedom from economic want, and freedom from harassment by police. With such a range of interpretations it might have taken considerable time for any administration to develop a strong or solid constituency for upholding human rights in foreign policy. Perhaps most significantly, however, about a third of those interviewed could not mention one example of what human rights meant to them.

Isolationism and related topics: The questions in Table

12 deal with a variety of issues broadly related to isolationism. In the 1976 surveys, questions dealt with intervention and military commitments. In 1977, the surveys focused instead on foreign trade and arm sales.

One common question in all ten cities did deal directly with general feelings of isolationism. All the respondents were asked whether the U.S. would be better off if "we just stayed home," a question used in several University of Michigan national election studies over the past twenty years. Fewer than one in three who expressed an opinion in our surveys agreed. Even fewer people in the 1976 surveys agreed that other countries of the world would be better off if the U.S. were to stay home.

Answers to the 1976 questions reveal a public supportive of keeping American troops in Europe and the Far East, but not by large margins. Moreover, other countries (even our allies) were seen as fair game for American espionage. But the public drew the line on secret interference in the political affairs in other countries by a more than 2-to-1 margin, even when those countries had Communist governments or were in conflict with Communist insurgents.

The 1977 surveys revealed strong protectionist sentiments despite widespread public feeling that foreign trade was necessary for our economic well-being. More people agreed than disagreed that we should keep foreign products out of our country to save American jobs, even if it meant spending more money for American products. Furthermore, many more respondents favored making it difficult for foreign companies to build factories in this country. While the surveys did not inquire into the reasons behind these protectionist replies, it is interesting to find the greatest support for construction of foreign-owned factories in the one city in the survey (Cleveland) that had attempted to attract foreign companies. Significantly, Cleveland was also the city that expressed a relatively high degree of support for general isolationism.

TABLE 12

OPINIONS ON ISOLATIONISM, INTERVENTIONISM, AND TRADE
(Exact question wording shown in Appendix A)

CITY MONTH SAMPLE SIZE (N =)	1976						1977					
	PITT. FEB. (299)	S. FR. MAR. (309)	PORT. MAR. (306)	MILW. APR. (292)	MINN. APR. (300)	TOTAL	L.A. MAY (300)	ST. L. SEPT. (315)	PORT. SEPT. (302)	CLEV. OCT. (301)	ATL. DEC. (301)	TOTAL
Position					*Percentage Indicating Acceptance*							
U.S. better off staying home	29%	27%	31%	45%	28%	32%	30%	28%	26%	35%	25%	29%
Rest of world better off if U.S. stayed home	17	27	28	35	23	26	NA†	NA	NA	NA	NA	NA
Bring troops home from Japan	29*	41	40	39	35	37	NA	NA	NA	NA	NA	NA
Bring troops home from Korea	33*	40	36	39	32	36	NA	NA	NA	NA	NA	NA
Bring troops home from Europe	34*	31	28	31	26	30	NA	NA	NA	NA	NA	NA
No spying on community	NA	15	13	15	18	12	NA	NA	NA	NA	NA	NA
No spying on troublemakers	NA	24	16	26	17	21	NA	NA	NA	NA	NA	NA
No spying on friendly countries	NA	44	34	45	38	40	NA	NA	NA	NA	NA	NA
No secret help; U.S. unfriendly country	NA	78	69	75	72	74	NA	NA	NA	NA	NA	NA
No secret help; U.S. unfriendly dictatorship	NA	70	60	NA	57	63	NA	NA	NA	NA	NA	NA
No secret help; U.S. Communist backed	NA	67	58	70	60	62	NA	NA	NA	NA	NA	NA
No secret help; U.S. Communists	NA	72	60	63	57	63	NA	NA	NA	NA	NA	NA
Economy OK without foreign trade	NA	NA	NA	NA	NA	NA	NA	31	19	31	25	27
Keep foreign products out to protect U.S. jobs	NA	NA	NA	NA	NA	NA	NA	54	42	55	44	49
Discourage foreign factories in U.S.	NA	NA	NA	NA	NA	NA	NA	50	38	32	35	38
U.S. should not sell any weapons to anyone	NA	NA	NA	NA	NA	NA	NA	26	NA	34	NA	NA
U.S. should sell to anyone who can pay	NA	NA	NA	NA	NA	NA	NA	12	NA	16	NA	NA

*Slightly different wording   †NA—Question not asked

Goals and Values: The first question in each city's questionnaire usually dealt with the respondent's general values and orientations toward certain goals of foreign policy. The goals included "stopping the spread of communism," "protecting the jobs of American workers," and "stopping wars between the smaller countries of the world." Respondents were asked to rate each goal as "very important," "somewhat important," or "not very important." Table 13 presents the proportion of respondents who rated each goal as very important in each of the ten cities surveyed.

Stopping the spread of dictatorships was a very important goal for 48 percent of the respondents in the 1976 set of five cities and for 49 percent in the 1977 set of five cities. However, in San Francisco (surveyed in 1976), only 36 percent rated stopping dictatorships as a very important goal while in Minnesota, 57 percent rated it as very important. Only 41 percent in San Francisco rated stopping the spread of communism very important compared to 74 percent in Minnesota.

On other goals, the citizens of San Francisco and Minnesota were much more in agreement: in stopping world hunger (74 to 75 percent), in helping less-developed countries (40 to 39 percent), in raising the U.S. standard of living (52 to 53 percent), and in keeping peace (73 to 79 percent). In general, the results of both sets of surveys suggest that foreign policy views in San Francisco were highly atypical. The lack of variation across the five 1977 cities is particularly striking. This is further indicated by responses to the other attitude questions in Tables 9-12. A considerable stability also exists in the responses across the two years of the study. In terms of the four comparable questions used, 51 percent of the Pittsburgh sample interviewed in January 1976 rated stopping dictatorships very important, compared to 47 percent of those in Atlanta interviewed in December 1977; in the case of stopping communism, the percentages were 68 and 69 percent; in helping less-devel-

TABLE 13

OPINIONS ON GENERAL ORIENTATIONS AND VALUES

CITY / MONTH / SAMPLE SIZE (N =)	1976						1977					
Position	PITT. FEB. (299)	S. FR. MAR. (309)	PORT. MAR. (306)	MILW. APR. (292)	MINN. APR. (300)	TOTAL	L.A. MAY (300)	ST. L. SEPT. (315)	PORT. SEPT. (302)	CLEV. OCT. (301)	ATL. DEC. (301)	TOTAL
						Percentage Indicating Agreement						
Stopping spread of dictatorships	51%	36%	46%	48%	57%	48%	52%	47%	48%	49%	47%	49%
Stopping spread of communism	68	41	62	68	74	62	66	66	62	68	69	66
Persuading other countries to be more democratic	37	23	29	26	36	30	NA†	NA	37	NA	NA	NA
Speaking against countries that violate human rights	NA	NA	NA	NA	NA	NA	64*	53	39*	58	51	54
Stopping world hunger	68	74	65	74	75	71	81	NA	77	NA	NA	NA
Giving food to countries where people are in need	NA	NA	NA	NA	NA	NA	NA	63	NA	61	60	61
Helping to raise the standard of living in LDCs	33	40	33	33	39	36	46	47	49	38	40	44
Raising U.S. standard of living	61	52	59	59	53	57	NA	NA	53	NA	NA	NA
Protecting American jobs	87	75	80	78	80	80	85	86	78	89	83	84
Keeping the U.S. most powerful	NA	NA	NA	NA	NA	NA	60	57	NA	63	60	60
Reducing the sale of military equipment to other countries	NA	NA	NA	NA	NA	NA	57	49	59	53	47	53
Encouraging business and trade with other countries	NA	NA	NA	NA	NA	NA	NA	54	NA	51	52	52
Stopping wars between small countries	32	18	26	40	28	29	NA	NA	38	NA	NA	NA
Protecting weaker countries	31	23	27	26	34	28	NA	NA	41	NA	NA	NA
Keeping peace in the world	74	73	77	77	79	74	89	NA	79	NA	NA	NA
Influencing other countries to agree to prevent wars	NA	NA	NA	NA	NA	NA	NA	79	NA	82	80	80
Making agreements with Russia to control nuclear weapons	NA	NA	NA	NA	NA	NA	78	76	NA	74	72	75

*Slightly different wording †NA—Question not asked NA—Question not asked (Exact question wording shown in Appendix A) oped countries, 33 and 40 percent; in protecting American jobs, 87 and 83 percent.

What might normally be regarded as a minor difference in wording accounted for a large difference in responses to a question asked in Los Angeles and Portland (see Table 13). In Los Angeles, respondents were asked about the goal of "persuading other countries to respect the human rights of their citizens," while in Portland, respondents were asked about "telling other countries to stop violating the human rights of their citizens." The lower aggression implied in the term *persuading* appears to have been responsible for the 64 percent "very important" rating in Los Angeles compared to only a 39 percent "very important" rating in Portland.

The questions in Table 13 generally converge in their portrayal of a public mainly concerned about the domestic consequences of foreign policy. The general goal or value that consistently aroused most support in both the 1976 and 1977 surveys was job protection for American workers. Substantial importance was also attached to two other "domestic" goals—raising the U.S. standard of living and making the U.S. the most powerful country in the world. Far more of the 1976 respondents were willing to rate raising the U.S. standard of living as "very important" than were willing to assign the same priority to helping the less-developed countries raise their standard of living.

Helping poorer countries develop was seen as less important in general than helping relieve immediate needs, such as hunger. However, here we began to encounter the types of ambiguity that can often be attributed to variations in question wording. This seems to be the most plausible explanation for the greater importance attached to "stopping world hunger" than to "giving food to countries where people don't have enough to eat."

But the statements dealing with war and peace seemed to generate consensus, no matter how we worded them. "Keeping world peace" achieved the second highest rating in the

1976 surveys, and when we changed the wording in the 1977 surveys to "influencing other countries to make agreements to prevent wars," it did not lose this standing; moreover, practically the same importance was attached to the related goal of "reaching nuclear agreements with the Soviet Union."

When such peace-keeping sentiments were translated into images of the U.S. as "world policeman," they received little support. The goals of stopping wars between smaller countries and protecting weaker countries against foreign aggression were at the bottom of the 1976 list. But almost two-thirds of the public in both 1976 and 1977 rated stopping communism as a very important goal of foreign policy. And this, it should be noted, was just before the Soviet and Cuban intervention in Africa.

In all ten cities, stopping the spread of communism was rated as considerably more important than stopping the spread of dictatorships, indicating that communist influence mattered to the public more than the fact that people had to live under authoritarian regimes. (As will be seen shortly, the two items were highly interrelated, however.) With the various differences in phrasing noted above, our "speaking out for human rights" item in the 1977 surveys was rated at the same level of importance as "stopping the spread of dictatorships."

Finally, Table 13 shows that in the 1977 surveys, the goals of reducing arms sales and encouraging foreign trade were rated at about the same level of importance as speaking out on human rights. It is clear, then, that more specific economic and political goals did not occupy the same level of concern in the public's consciousness as domestic welfare and military preparedness.

Question Wording Changes

While we were unable in the course of our studies to carry out actual experiments in question wording, we did note changes in responses from city to city as a result of changes in wording. (We noted few location differences, however, when the same questions were asked.) As the following examples from Tables 9-13 show, these word changes often appeared to produce somewhat inconsistent results:

• While 46 percent of those sampled in 1976 said our government should have criticized the Soviet Union for its human rights violations, only 16 percent chose it as a more important goal than either nuclear arms agreements or trade with the Soviet Union. (Table 9 and Table 11)

• While only 48 percent felt our government should criticize countries that violated the human rights of their citizens, 63 percent felt we should refuse to do business with such countries—even if the U.S. lost business as a result. (Table 11)

Los Angeles respondents (as noted above) readily approved of "persuasion" in advocacy of human rights while the Portland sample resisted the idea of "telling" other countries to stop rights violations.

• While 71 percent in the 1976 polls (and 81 percent in Los Angeles and 77 percent in Portland in the 1977 polls) rated "stopping world hunger" as a very important goal, only 61 percent in the remaining three 1977 cities attached the same importance to giving food to countries with undernourished populations. (Table 13)

On first glance, post hoc explanations for these "inconsistencies" are not difficult to construct. Compared with reducing the risk of nuclear war, human rights are obviously of second order importance. Enough people seem opposed to foreign trade in general that suggesting restrictions on officials who persecute their citizenry stiffens opposition to foreign trade. The term *persuading* is gentle and vague; the words *telling* or *speaking up* are harsher. *Giving* food implies costs and actions that are not suggested by a general proposal to stop world hunger.

These examples illustrate the frustration we experienced

at being unable to anticipate when question wording factors would come into play. Our attempts to represent public thinking on a complicated issue with a single question were equally trying. They reinforced our conviction that multiple questions, using multiple formats, are necessary to plumb the complexities of public opinion adequately. But with all their limitations, our surveys agree remarkably well with national surveys on the same topics.

Comparison with Similar Surveys

We were able to compare our results for one question asked in the ten-city study with a fully national data source, the Center for Political Studies (CPS) at the University of Michigan. The CPS conducted its interviews personally rather than by telephone and was able to do so with a much lower rate of refusal than our study. The question involved, "This country would be much better off if we stayed home and did not concern ourselves with problems in other parts of the world," was often used in these Michigan election studies. The results from the 1976 CPS study were virtually identical to the overall response from our ten sites in 1976-77.

Thirty-one percent of respondents in our ten-city sample agreed with the statement compared to 30 percent in the CPS study; 64 percent disagreed in both studies; the remaining 6 percent in the CPS study and 5 percent in our study fell in the various "no opinion" categories.

The two data sets also showed remarkable convergences in the relations of question responses to respondents' age and education. In the CPS study, 59 percent of those with a grade school education agreed with the statement compared to only 10 percent of college graduates; in our study, the respective proportions were 55 and 17 percent. Twenty-three percent of those aged eighteen to twenty-four in the CPS study agreed with the statement and that figure gradually increased to 39 percent for those who were aged sixty and above. In our study, the respective proportions were 25 percent and 40 percent.

Our conclusions also bear a strong resemblance to those gained from a comprehensive public opinion study conducted in 1974 for the Chicago Council on Foreign Relations. Our studies repeated many of the questions in this study, with some wording changes. The Council's study utilized a national sample of 1,513 respondents interviewed by the Louis Harris Organization.

It is instructive to compare verbatim conclusions from the Council's final report that bear on each of the topics discussed in our findings:

East-West Relations: Hostility toward some of the communist nations . . . has gone down. For example 58% of the public believes that the U.S. and the U.S.S.R. can reach agreements to keep peace.

Communism is still a threatening phenomenon to at least a substantial minority of the population, even if we seem to have stabilized our relations with some particular communist countries.

. . . two-thirds of the public want to do so [expand trade with the Soviet Union] . . . .[4]

Third World: The public is also willing to cut U.S. food consumption (but not accept higher prices) to help poor countries. . . . Humanitarian and emergency aid are strongly supported.

Finally, there was some evidence that average Americans were skeptical about how much benefit economic aid actually brings to the intended recipients.

Indeed most of the American public (52% with 38% opposing) generally favored giving economic aid to other nations for purposes of economic development and technical assistance . . . and a strong majority, 79%, of the public declared that it would favor the giving of economic aid if they could be shown that it ended up helping the people of those countries.[5]

Human Rights: Two-thirds of the American public believe that the U.S. should put pressure on countries which systematically violate basic human rights.

When attitudes toward the violation of human rights are probed in the abstract, support for the human rights position is substantial . . . when it comes to specifics, the public response is less clear.[6]

Isolationism and Related Matters: Even so, there is little sentiment among the American public for a retreat from the world.

Two-thirds of the American public show a great belief that "the United States should play an active role in the world."

When asked whether the secret political operations of the CIA should be expanded, cut back, or kept about the same . . . the national sample . . . tended to favor cutbacks.

Foreign military sales are less unpopular than military aid, but only 35% of the public *(favors such sales).*[7]

Moreover, in 1978, Rielly replicated this national study and reached substantially the same conclusions.

To be sure, some things had changed between 1974 and 1978, the period in which our surveys were conducted. There was a decline in public support for economic aid in general (but only by 6 percentage points). An increased wariness about U.S.-Soviet relations was reflected in the increased interest in defense spending. This evidence of a shift toward heightened self-interest in 1978, however, was still not sufficient to negate any of the general conclusions reached in the 1974 study.[8]

Finally, the rankings of foreign policy goals and values in our 1976-77 surveys converge with those used in the Chicago Council national studies, and the questions used in both are strikingly similar.

The public in the 1974 Chicago Council survey put world peace and job protection for American workers at the top of the list, much as it did in the ten-city survey. Arms control, world hunger, and containment of communism were in the middle of the priority list; and helping less-developed countries, protecting weaker countries, and bringing democracy to other nations were at the bottom of the list. In our 1976-77 surveys and in the 1978 Chicago Council study, protecting the jobs of American workers had moved ahead of world peace as an important policy goal.[9]

Our conclusions on foreign aid and Third World attitudes also dovetail with a 1972 comprehensive survey done for the Overseas Development Council (OCD). The OCD survey focused on the single topic of foreign aid and was able to document, through a variety of both closed-and open-ended questions, that "public support for the idea of giving U.S. assistance to underdeveloped countries is at an historic high." But it found, much as our study and the Chicago Council study found, that the public had grave misgivings about the present means of distributing aid and was more open to new efforts directed through private agencies. As the report put it: "The public appears to consider voluntary agencies more reliable assistance channels than government aid programs." The 1972 OCD study was also able to document more directly than our surveys that the public felt that need should be given a higher priority than potential for self-sufficiency in providing aid to the Third World. "Public support," the report said, "is strongest to alleviate such basic problems as hunger and malnutrition, disease, and illiteracy. Americans consider aid in these areas to be more direct, its results more visible, and its dispersal less likely to meet with corruption."[10]

Relationships with Other Variables

Our discussion of survey results has thus far concentrated on the overall "univariate," or marginal, distributions of replies for the entire public. On many policy issues, however, it is more important to understand "bivariate" distributions; that is, the relationships between opinions and respondents' personal backgrounds or the relationships between the opinions of a given sector of the public on a number of issues. If, for example, substantial opposition to a policy comes from highly educated people, policy makers are likely to encounter a vocal and influential resistance to pursuit of that policy. Opposition by younger people to military proposals may mean greater difficulty in winning their support or recruiting their participation in action resulting from such policies.

Our surveys showed that both young and highly educated respondents were more likely to support foreign aid, to take more conciliatory positions toward the Soviet Union, and to reject isolationist sentiments. In some instances, the age effect predominated. In the case of trust of the Soviet Union, younger people differed from older people more often than better-educated people differed from less-educated people. However, on issues such as isolationism or stopping communism educational differences predominated.

A common and more interesting age/education pattern emerged for several other questions—those regarding waste in foreign aid, keeping militarily ahead of the Soviet Union, and criticism of human rights violations abroad. Here the combination produced offsetting results. The combination of high school dropouts and young people (under thirty years) produced the same patterns of opinion as the combination of people with some college education and older people (over fifty years). In general, a shift toward a better-educated adult public would lead one to expect less support for isolationist and "hard-line" foreign policies. But, these demographic shifts are hardly likely to be revolutionary, nor as visible as they were in the 1960s.

The statistical basis for these observations is given in Appendix B, where we show and discuss differences by age and by education for each of our foreign policy questions. This analysis employs a special "multivariate" technique to calculate age effects independently of education effects, i.e., effects corrected for the fact that younger people are better-educated than older people even though both groups share other social characteristics.

Differences in opinion due to four of these other social characteristics were much less significant than for age or education. Women tended to endorse more isolationist and anti-Communist sentiments than men, but were also more supportive of certain aspects of foreign aid. Blacks were less supportive of criticisms of human rights violations in other countries than were whites, and took slightly more militaristic and isolationist positions than whites. Except for one issue, on which Independents differed with Republicans and Democrats, differences by political party identification were almost nonexistent. In our earlier studies, income was a factor in only one question: Lower income groups tended to be more isolationist, even after our analysis was adjusted to account for generally higher levels of education among high income groups.

The relationships between education, age, and the other factors were generally found in each city's survey when the surveys were examined independently—even though the sample sizes for many of the comparison groups (i.e., blacks, under thirty year olds) were well below 100 in each city. The same replication held true for relationships between the attitudes themselves, as shown in Appendix D.

The basis of Appendix D is a computer technique called "factor analysis" that identifies the major coherent themes that run through a set of items. There was, moreover, a coalescence of the findings about attitudes in Appendix D and the findings of Appendix B regarding background factors, as well as with factor analyses done on the national data collected by the Chicago Council. The most important policy lesson from the Appendix B material, however, is how difficult it is to assume that the public can be divided into popular categories like liberals or conservatives (or hard-liners or soft-hearteds) on matters of foreign policy.

The Informed Public

We have noted how some policy makers weigh opinions of "elites" or their acquaintances more heavily than those of the public. Given the well-documented fact that the public is ill informed on foreign affairs (Lane and Sears, 1964; Robinson, 1966; Cohen, 1973), a plausible argument can be made for conducting separate examinations of those population groups that are highly interested or well informed about the issues involved.[11]

These are the groups we surveyed at the town meetings. Although any citizen who wished could attend the meetings and join in the discussions, the format virtually ensured that attendance would be limited to those with a relatively strong interest in foreign policy.

A determined attempt was made by the coordinating organization in each community to convene a very wide representation of organizations and individuals concerned about foreign policy and its implications. The meeting agenda was publicized well in advance through the mass media in each community. It was, in this sense, a genuine public meeting.

Who then came to the meetings, and how well did their views represent the community as a whole? To what extent could the State Department officials feel that they had engaged in a fully public dialogue in each community? In an attempt to answer these questions, we interviewed attendees in two of the cities, Pittsburgh and Cleveland, asking them the same questions we had asked the public in the telephone polls.

We interviewed thirty-five appointed discussion leaders just before the February 1976 town meeting in Pittsburgh. In Cleveland, we interviewed not only the seventeen discussion leaders for the November 1977 meeting, but 120 members of the audience as well. To the extent we could, we sampled the attending public by systematic random procedures applied on the basis of the order in which they entered each of the four discussion rooms. Approximately three-quarters of those who were handed a questionnaire completed and returned it to our field workers.

The comparisons between the public and town meeting participants in the two communities are presented in Tables 14 and 15. Table 14 reveals that the Pittsburgh public responses differed significantly (usually by more than 20 percentage points) from responses by meeting participants on most of the thirty-three questions asked of the two samples. They differed most on their support for activist, interventionist activities by the government—"elite" participants were much more likely to support keeping our troops overseas and engaging in interventionist activities in other countries. They felt strongly that we have a responsibility to keep peace in the world. In a related fashion, they were less likely to attach much importance to the domestic consequences of foreign policy—protecting the jobs of American workers or raising our own standard of living. It should be noted that this is also part of a tendency on the part of this "elite" to rate all the general goals or values of foreign policy as less important than did the public as a whole.

On East-West issues the town meeting discussion leaders were much more open than the public to trade with the Soviet Union, and to more liberal terms on such trade. While they attached much less importance to the goal of stopping communism in general, they were just as wary of the Soviet Union; like the general public, two-thirds agreed that the United States could not trust the U.S.S.R. to live up to its agreements. And while they were much less likely to feel that we should keep ahead of the Soviet Union militarily, they were not less likely to feel that we should increase our military and defense budgets.

On Third World issues, this elite sample's views also diverged widely from those of the public. Here again the leadership group took a much more activist stance, being consistently more in favor of aid and more likely to agree that the U.S. had failed to pay a fair price for raw materials from Third World countries. In contrast to the public, a majority favored the principle of "triage" being applied, that is helping those in the Third World most likely to attain self-sufficiency rather than those most needy. In contrast, this elite group also attached relatively more importance to the goals dealing with world hunger and aid to developing countries.

While no direct questions on human rights were included in this phase of our surveys, the elite groups were far less likely than the general public to endorse the survey statements dealing with the promotion of democracy abroad—stopping the spread of dictatorships or using trade as a means of forcing the Soviet Union into democratic reforms.

The elite unanimously rejected the statements dealing with isolationist sentiments (although some elite respondents did feel that other countries in the world might be better off if we were to stay home). The discussion leaders' predilection for a more activist and interventionist posture in foreign affairs can be detected in their support for foreign aid and for domestic aspects of foreign policy; they were far less likely than the public to see American leaders as inattentive to what U.S. policies cost the American people.

These attitude patterns are in line with what one would expect from a comparison of a well-educated sample and one that is less well educated. The median educational achievement of our elite sample was a college degree, a level of education attained by only about 20 percent of the Pittsburgh public interviewed by telephone. We have portrayed the views of this college graduate subpublic of 20 percent in the center column of Table 14.

This adjustment does narrow the gap between the public and the elite on almost every issue in the expected direction. In other words, the differences just described as elite-related are education-related as well. On the question of helping

TABLE 14

PITTSBURGH MASS VS. ELITE FOREIGN POLICY ATTITUDES
(January 1976)

	GENERAL PUBLIC		ELITE (TOWN MEETING)
	Total (N=340)	College Educated (N=58)	Discussion Leaders (N=35)
Position	*Percentage Indicating Acceptance*		
East-West Relations			
U.S. should spend more on military	23%	18%	20%
Keep well ahead of Russia militarily	52	33	29
U.S. cannot trust Russians	66	64	66
Favor U.S.-Soviet trade	61	83	88
Extend Russian trade credit	16	24	51
Oppose using Russian trade for democratic pressure	47	58	74
Third World Relations			
U.S. should give aid, even if they don't stand for same things	39	42	80
U.S. should give aid only to countries that help us	44	35	34
U.S. should give aid only to democracies	33	19	9
U.S. has not paid fair price for raw materials from less-developed countries	17	36	46
U.S. should help less-developed countries	63	77	92
Personally willing to help people in less-developed countries	66	80	100
Help countries on need rather than on self-sufficiency	58	55	33
Intervention			
U.S. should keep troops in Japan	57	70	89
U.S. should engage in spying	72	85	100

	GENERAL PUBLIC		ELITE (TOWN MEETING)
	Total (N=340)	College Educated (N=58)	Discussion Leaders (N=35)
Position			
U.S. should influence events in other countries	29	38	54
U.S. has responsibility to keep peace	72	75	83
U.S. better off by staying home (disagree)	67	74	100
Rest of world better off if U.S. stays home (disagree)	73	84	93
U.S. ally only with democracies	26	20	3
Other			
U.S. leaders don't care what we think	79	68	40
Values	*Percentage Indicating "Very Important"*		
Raise our own standard of living	60	57	26
Protect American jobs	87	77	49
Keep our own interests first	64	57	34
Having as little to do with other countries	12	14	0
Stop world hunger	73	74	74
Help less-developed countries	36	40	43
Protect weaker countries against aggression	35	36	23
Stop wars between smaller countries	35	38	34
Keep peace in the world	77	68	40
Persuade other countries to be democratic	44	46	23
Stop the spread of dictatorships	50	41	26
Stop the spread of communism	64	49	29

95

Third World countries, for example, 77 percent of the college graduates in Pittsburgh felt we should, compared to 63 percent for the Pittsburgh public as a whole; 83 percent of college graduates in the Pittsburgh telephone sample favored U.S.-Soviet trade compared to only 61 percent of the larger public; and only 49 percent of college graduates saw stopping communism as a very important goal, compared to 64 percent of the public as a whole. These are examples of significant education-related differences.

Nonetheless, it is just as clear that this "education effect" does not explain all of the elite-mass difference. On most questions, the college-educated subpublic stands *between* the elite and the general public. On many questions though, the distance between the college-educated and the mass public is less than the midpoint between the elite and the public as a whole: On stopping the spread of communism, the gap between the college educated and the rest of the public is 15 percent (64 – 49 percent) compared to 35 percent (64 – 29 percent) for the elite-public difference. For stopping the spread of dictatorships, the college-public difference is 9 percent, the elite-public difference 24 percent. On general isolationism, the college-public gap is 7 percent, the elite-public gap 33 percent. On Third World countries 14 percent compared to 29 percent; on triage the college-public gap is only 3 percent compared to 25 percent for the elite-public gap. It is clear then that these discussion leaders in Pittsburgh were a highly distinctive group in their support of activist foreign policies, one that is only partially explainable by equalizing the Pittsburgh public sample in terms of comparable levels of education.

Although not as pronounced, much the same pattern is repeated for the Cleveland public-versus-elite differences as well. The data are shown in Table 15, with the town meeting participants' responses being shown separately from the discussion leaders (in parentheses); questions that are repeats of those used in Pittsburgh are noted with an asterisk. The following differences can be observed:

East-West: Town meeting participants were again less concerned about being militarily ahead of the Soviet Union and stopping the spread of communism, but just as wary of trusting the Soviet Union. Similar to the Pittsburgh leaders' openness to Russian trade, the Cleveland town meeting participants were more in favor of nuclear arms agreements with the Soviet Union (note below that they were also more in favor of criticizing the Soviet Union for its human rights violations).

Third World: Participants again saw aid to the Third World as more important than did the public and were more sympathetic to the view that the less-developed countries do not receive fair prices for their raw materials.

Human Rights: While more critical of human rights violations by the Soviet Union and placing more importance on speaking up for human rights, town meeting participants placed no more importance on the goals of stopping the spread of dictatorships or promoting democracy abroad. Participants were, moreover, much less likely to agree that the U.S. should refuse to do business with human rights violators. (Although not shown in Table 14, the leaders were far more likely than the public to suggest a U.N. condemnation of South Africa for its human rights violations, but no more likely to support trade or arms embargoes on that country.)

Isolationism: Again the same rejection of isolationist and self-interest themes was evident among the town meeting participants in Cleveland. There was also more encouragement for foreign trade among the participants but also more support for reduced arms sales. Perhaps the most surprising result in Table 14 in light of the general similarity to the Pittsburgh results is that the Cleveland town meeting participants were hardly more open to foreign companies building factories in this country than the general public.

Finally, like the Pittsburgh participants, those in Cleveland were much less likely than the public to feel that U.S. leaders were unconcerned with the public's views on foreign policy.

TABLE 15

CLEVELAND MASS VS. ELITE FOREIGN POLICY ATTITUDES
(November 1977)

	GENERAL PUBLIC		ELITE (TOWN MEETING)	
Position	Total (N=304)	College (N=56)	Total (N=120)	Discussion Leaders (N=17)
	Percentage Indicating Acceptance			
East-West Relations				
*U.S. cannot trust Russians	66%	55%	59%	36%
*Keep well ahead of Russia militarily	51	39	34	36
Favor U.S.-Russia agreements on nuclear power	52	76	64	80
Third World Relations				
*U.S. should help less-developed countries	54	62	88	100
*U.S. has not paid fair price for raw materials from less-developed countries	17	30	46	46
Human Rights				
Refuse business with human rights violators	74	63	46	40
Isolationism				
*U.S. better off by staying home	34	14	6	0
U.S. arms sales too much	49	65	77	85
Make it easy for foreign countries to build in U.S.	36	45	34	53

	GENERAL PUBLIC		ELITE (TOWN MEETING)	
	Total (N=304)	College (N=56)	Total (N=120)	Discussion Leaders (N=17)
Values				
*Protect American jobs	86	76	54	33
*Help less-developed countries	48	51	60	75
*Persuade other countries to be democratic	50	42	49	57
*Stop the spread of dictatorships	54	39	42	33
*Stop the spread of communism	64	49	41	33
Speak up on human rights	50	61	57	43
Encourage foreign business and trade	52	76	65	73
Other				
*U.S. leaders don't care what we think	53	29	30	13

*Repeat of question used in Pittsburgh.

While the college-educated public in Cleveland was not as consistent as in Pittsburgh in endorsing positons between elite and mass opinion, Table 15 does represent an impressive replication of the results found in Pittsburgh. In addition, while the opinion polls in the two communities did indicate there to be a somewhat more conservative, hard-line, or isolationist attitude in these cities than in other cities, the differences were not that great. Still, it would have been interesting to measure differences between the public and elite opinion in cities like San Francisco or Portland, where the foreign policy leadership may have markedly different opinions that those in Pittsburgh and Cleveland.

It is obvious, however, that our public opinion survey

results did perform the function that we had anticipated: They demonstrated differences between general and informed public orientations. In few ways could the views of the participants in the town meetings be considered representative of the communities in which they were held. Nor could the views of participants be considered homogeneous. The 120 participants in the Cleveland meeting also differed widely depending on which of the four "workshops" they decided to attend, as shown in Appendix C.

The results in Tables 14 and 15 should be read with special care by decision makers who depend on *volunteer* samples for audience or public response. These include members of Congress whose mail surveys depend on constituents willing to take time and effort to reply, newspaper editors who treat their mail as if it accurately represents what is on the public's mind and television producers so sensitive to telephone and mail reactions that one viewer's reaction is seen as reflecting the thoughts of a thousand others. Most local politicians probably realize that few people come to local hearings or council meetings without some vested interest to defend, and that the spectators of the meeting are hardly representative of the community as a whole. However, the same limitation should be recognized in any other volunteer sample encountered by policy makers.

Notes

1. The full random digit method would involve calling a large quantity of nonworking exchanges. In order to eliminate as many nonworking telephone numbers as possible, the telephone directory was used to identify exchanges that were most likely to be in use. These directory numbers were then used as the base for generating telephone numbers at random.

2. Although the survey included a state-wide sample (Minnesota), for convenience we will refer to the study as a ten-city survey.

3. A question asked only in Portland in 1977 indicated that a third of those favoring trade did oppose selling computers to the Soviet Union, but almost all favored selling appliances to them.

4. John E. Rielly, *American Public Opinion and U.S. Foreign Policy 1975* (Chicago: The Chicago Council on Foreign Relations, 1975), pp. 7, 22.

5. Ibid., pp. 7, 27.

6. Ibid., pp. 7, 22.

7. Ibid., pp. 5-7, 23.

8. The 1974 Chicago Council study was able to probe two points in more detail than our study.

a) Despite approval for the principle of foreign aid, a "majority of Americans [56 percent] favored cutting back on economic aid," and 24 percent named it as one of the first two or three federal programs (out of thirteen) that should be cut back; and on another aspect of aid, "most Americans rated our relations with developing nations as being less important, on the whole, than relations with industrialized nations, both western and Communist."

b) Despite the almost 5-to-1 support for cutting back rather than expanding the political operations of the CIA (particularly after the unpopular CIA intervention in Chile), 43 percent of the public agreed the CIA should "work inside other countries to try to strengthen those elements that serve the interests of the United States and to weaken those forces that work against the interests of the U.S." compared to only 26 percent who said it should not.

9. However, in the 1978 study, two new foreign policy goals, "keeping up the value of the dollar" and "securing adequate energy supplies," rated higher than protecting American jobs. Both those goals, of course, further reinforce the importance of domestic values in foreign policy.

10. Paul Laudicina, *World Poverty and Development: A Survey of American Opinion* (Washington, DC: Overseas Development Council, 1974), pp. 4-5.

11. This was often suggested, for example, during the Vietnam War, because it was widely presumed that the informed public would be the one most opposed to our involvement there—an expectation that generally was not borne out by breakdowns of poll data by education or information level (Converse and Schuman, 1970; Verba et al., 1970; Mueller, 1973).

6 *Question Framing*

PERHAPS NO STEP IN THE PROCESS of survey research and analysis is more important than the method of framing questions. In no other phase of polling is there greater potential for "bias" or ambiguity. Reputable pollsters, of course, work diligently to avoid bias in their questions because their long-term credibility depends on it. But despite their efforts, bias invariably arises in the form of unintended distortions and ambiguities, a function of the almost limitless choices available in preparing questions.

Although the wording of poll questions has become a widespread professional concern, until recently little research had been conducted to guide survey practitioners in improving their question framing. The need for such guidance was recognized as early as 1936, when three-quarters of a sample of opinion researchers cited "improperly worded questionnaires" as the most frequent criticism of opinion research. More than a decade later, upon completing their monumental wartime study of *The American Soldier,* the pioneering social scientist Samuel Stouffer and his colleagues concluded that "variation attributable to different ways of wording questions" was the chief source of bias in research.[1] Shortly thereafter, poll question expert Stanley Payne offered his diagnosis of the same problem: "Probably the reason that the question worder hasn't done more to advance this phase of research is that he just doesn't exist, at least not as a specialist."[2]

Subsequent lack of progress in the field is in part due to

the many institutional obstacles that poll researchers encounter. Moreover, it is not possible to conduct public opinion research under ideal scientific circumstances. In medical research, two "treatments" can be tested under the same conditions. But in a single survey, an opinion researcher cannot offer two similar versions of a question to the same respondent. To do so would risk alienating respondents, and one's reaction to the first question is very likely to influence one's reaction to the second.

An alternative approach to this problem involves the random assignment "split halves" or "split ballot" technique. With this method, sample respondents are randomly divided into two groups. One half is asked one version of each question and the other half, a second version. If 60 percent of the first random group gives a "pro" response while only 10 percent of the second group gives a "pro" response, one has a reasonably scientific basis for concluding that the question framing used for the two groups is responsible for the difference.

Recently there have been several such experimental studies of question framing. While the results of these studies hardly explain all of the problems we noted in chapter 4, they do represent significant progress in this essential aspect of polling. They provide a far better framework than our post hoc speculations for interpreting the divergent results in chapter 4. Therefore, we must see what has been learned from this research.

Our discussion of question framing will deal with the options that arise under the typical polling situation, where the opportunity exists to ask only one or two questions and where space and time limitations may preclude methodological checks on the reliability and validity of questions.[3]

Options

Recent experiments in question framing have focused on eight available options. The first four options deal with the format of questions. A format is selected for its ability to minimize the discomfort of the interview situation by providing simple options for declining to answer, avoiding automatic yea or nay saying, or revealing the orientation of the questioner. (The reader will note in the following examples that the difference between each two question formats has been italicized.)

1. Should one include a "Don't know" or "No opinion" filter to provide respondents with a comfortable opportunity to indicate their lack of familiarity with an issue? Filtering permits a clear separation between "informed" and "uninformed" opinion, a particularly useful distinction for foreign policy issues where few respondents can respond in terms of their personal experiences.

   Example: *Unfiltered:* "Do you think the United Nations has been doing a good job or a poor job in dealing with the problems it has had to face?"

   Filtered: "Do you think the United Nations has been doing a good job or a poor job in dealing with the problems it has had to face—*or haven't you followed this closely enough to have an opinion?*"

2. Should one give respondents two contrasting opinion options or three (or more) options so that respondents with middle-of-the-road attitudes can express such feelings? This distinction is important particularly when the survey analyst wishes to ascertain whether the respondents are leaning one way or the other or whether they have more neutral opinions.

   Example: *Two option:* "Do you think the United

Nations has been doing a good job or a poor job in dealing with the questions it has had to face?"

Three option: "Do you think the United Nations has been doing a good job, *a fair job*, or a poor job in dealing with the problems it has had to face?"

3. Should one use a balanced alternative (or forced choice) format rather than an "agree-disagree" (or approve-disapprove," "yes-no," etc.) format to allow respondents to see or appreciate both sides of an issue that are involved? Again, the balanced alternative approach answers the need to provide a more comfortable opportunity for disagreement on the part of the respondent.

Example: *Agree-disagree:* "The United Nations has been doing a good job in dealing with the problems it has had to face. Do you agree or disagree?"

Balanced alternative: "Some people feel that the
(Forced choice) United Nations has been doing a good job in dealing with the problems it has had to face, *while other people feel that the United Nations has been doing a poor job in dealing with the problems it has had to face. Which is closer to your opinion?"*

4. Should one use open-ended questions to allow respondents to express opinions from their own frame of reference? While open-ended questions give the respondent

105

greater freedom of expression, the cost of training interviewers and coding responses for analysis is far greater than for closed-ended questions.

Example: *Closed-ended:* "Do you think the United Nations is doing a good job or a poor job in dealing with the problems it has had to face?"

   Open-ended: "*What kind of job* do you think the United Nations is doing in dealing with the problems it has had to face?"

5. Where should one best place the question in the flow of the questionnaire? The "context" in which a question appears can be important, particularly in terms of the questions that precede it. One might expect more negative reactions to the United Nations question, for example, if it were preceded by several questions on other world problems or on how well U.S. tax money is spent than if it were preceded by questions on unrelated topics or optimistic foreign events.

6. In what order should response options be put? Given a two-sided issue, will more people agree if side A is presented first, or if side B is presented first? If there is a middle alternative, should it be presented second or third (or first)?

Example: *Order A:* "Do you think the United Nations has been doing a good job, a fair job, or a poor job in dealing with the problems it has had to face?"

   Order B: "Do you think the United Nations has been doing a

good job, *a poor job, or a
fair job* in dealing with the
problems it has had to
face?"

7. Should one provide respondents with information on the
   issue or not? Providing information has the advantage of
   jogging the respondent's memory in many cases but the
   disadvantage of over-simplifying all the information that
   may be available.

   Example: *Without* "Do you think the United
          information: Nations has been doing a
                    good job or a poor job in
                    dealing with the problems
                    it has had to face?

          With "*As you probably know,
          information: this past year the United
                    Nations has passed the
                    Zionist resolution, sent a
                    peace-keeping mission to
                    the Middle East and has
                    been involved in negotia-
                    tions in Africa.* Do you
                    think the United Nations
                    has been doing a good job
                    or a poor job in dealing
                    with the problems it has
                    had to face?"

8. Should one ask respondents about the strength or ex-
   tremity of their opinions? In this way, it would be possible
   to identify the size of the (usual) minorities with strongly
   held opinions on any issue.

   Example: *Without* "Do you think the United
          extreme Nations has been doing a
          responses: good job or a poor job in

	dealing with the problems it has had to face?"
With extreme responses:	"Do you think the United Nations has been doing a *very good job*, a good job, a poor job or a *very poor job* in dealing with the problems it has had to face?"

These eight options and the questions they raise provide an endless source of variations in question framing. But there are two even more pervasive problems that arise in question construction: (9) deciding what aspect of a question to focus on and (10) deciding what specific words to use to phrase the question. In the first case, for example, is the primary aim to evaluate the U.N.'s overall performance as an organization or to assess public sentiment about withdrawing from it? In the second, what specific words or phrases should the pollster choose to present the issues realistically and without bias? Figure 2 offers a step-by-step program to help researchers decide on both the appropriate context and wording of their questionnaires.

FIGURE 2

CONSTRUCTING AND ORDERING QUESTIONS

Step 1.   What is the issue? (e.g., the SALT II Treaty)

Step 2.   Who will be sampled?
    a) The mass public
    b) The informed public
    c) Political "influentials" and elites
    d) Those most affected by the Treaty

Step 3.   What specific aspects of the issue will be examined?
    a) Support for the principle of the Treaty
    b) Advantages of the Treaty
    c) Beneficiaries

Step 4. What questions will precede those on each aspect of the issue?
  a) None—they will lead off the interview
  b) Unrelated questions
  c) Related questions

Step 5. Should information about the issue be implied or included in the question itself?
  a) None, neither implicit nor explicit
  b) Implicit information (e.g., "The SALT II Treaty is being considered.")
  c) Explicit information (e.g., "As you may know, the Treaty provides x, y, and z.")

Step 6. Should a "Don't Know" or "No Opinion" filter be provided (mainly for surveys of mass publics)?
  a) "Do you approve or disapprove of x?"
  b) "Do you approve or disapprove of x, or haven't you heard enough about x to have an opinion?"

Step 7. Are you more interested in whether people feel one way or the other about the issue (closed-ended question) or about how they approach and perceive the issue (open-ended question)?
  a) "Do you approve or disapprove of x?"
  b) "There has been a lot of talk about x. How do you feel about x? What things do you like? What things don't you like?"

Step 8. If closed-ended: Should questions be put in agree-disagree (or yes-no) format or in terms of forced-choice or balanced alternatives?
  a) "Do you approve or disapprove of x?"
  b) "Do you approve of x or of y?"
  c) "Some people say that x is better because . . . . Other people say that y is better because . . . . How do you feel?"

Step 9. If multiple option: In which order should the options

be presented?
   a) "Do you prefer *x* or prefer *y*?"
   b) "Do you prefer *y* or prefer *x*?"

Step 10. If multiple option: Should two contrasting sides of an issue be presented, or should there also be a middle alternative?

Step 11. If closed-ended: Should a strength-of-opinion question be asked?
   a) "How strongly do you feel about this, *very strongly* or *not very strongly*?"

Step 12. Select final wording. Wording should be considered throughout, but the format must be selected before the question can be formulated exactly.

Most of the discussion thus far has centered on how question framing options affect the distribution of public opinion on an issue. But, simple division of opinion is not the only matter of concern to poll analysts. While a particular question format may be best for describing the pro-con distribution of opinion, it may be less useful for identifying consistencies or trends in public opinion. In general, researchers have considered how variations in question framing affect poll results on three criteria other than the simple pro-con distribution of opinion.

1. *Showing the differences between various groups (or subpublics) in the population.* Do younger people or older people have more favorable attitudes? Do men and women feel differently on the issue? On what aspects do educated and less-educated people evaluate the issues similarly and on what issues do they differ? In other words, depending on how the questions are framed, do we narrow or widen the differences between age or education subpublics?

2. *Describing the consistencies in public opinion.* Which

questions provide the most *reliability;* that is, produce consistently pro (or con) responses. Which questions provide the most *validity* by identifying people whose opinion is consistent with some behavior—such as voting or signing a petition or expressing an opinion to another person?

3. *Showing trends across time.* Which ways of framing questions best identify shifts in public opinion as events and participants in the foreign policy environment change? Which questions tap long-term orientations and which only short-term responses to events?

In the following review of research on the framing of survey questions we will use these four criteria to evaluate the eight options on format development.

1. Opinion Filtering

In their pioneering set of experiments on opinion filtering, Schuman and Presser (1978) found that explicitly presenting respondents with the "Don't know" or "No opinion" option did result in substantially more "Don't know" (DK) responses than when it was not offered. The increased proportion of DK responses from the six questions included in their experiment was between 20 and 25 percent, whether the questions dealt with remote foreign affairs (e.g., government in Portugal) or with more familiar domestic issues.

However, the overall distribution of pro-con opinion did not seem affected in the process: The proportion of pro versus con opinions remained roughly the same whether the filter option was offered or not. This resulted from those in the "no filter" situation splitting their opinions (or "psuedo-opinions") in roughly the same proportion as those who did express an opinion in the situation with a filtered question. In other words, if one obtained a 2-to-1 division of opinion among those choosing to answer the filtered questions, that same 2-to-1 division was found in the unfiltered version of the question. Schuman and Presser thus concluded, "Once

DK responses are excluded from both forms, univariate proportions are generally unaffected by the form." [4]

They also found little difference in filtered and unfiltered questions in their relation to background factors—the second of our criteria:

> There seems to be little effect of floating (i.e., choosing DK when offered, but not volunteering it if not offered) on the relations between attitude items and standard background factors. [5]

They were particularly surprised to find that "education is not involved, or is involved only to a minor extent," since they had expected less-educated people to feel more pressured to offer opinions in the unfiltered condition.

However, they did find differences in relation to associations with other opinion questions. But the effect was not always consistent. In some instances, the filtered question produced higher correlations with other questions than the unfiltered version, but in other instances it produced lower correlations.

In 1980, Bishop and his associates attempted to replicate and make generalizations from these experimental results of Schuman and Presser. While their questions were different and their sample sizes smaller and more local, Bishop et al. found that the Schuman-Presser results did not agree with their findings. For example, they found less than a 10 percentage point differential among the respondents in their samples choosing the filtered DK option on one racial opinion question and over a 40 percentage point differential in choosing the DK option on two items dealing with somewhat obscure foreign affairs issues. [6] The difference between these findings and the consistent 20 to 25 percent range in Schuman and Presser's experiments seems plausible given the usually greater public interest, personal experience, and familiarity with racial issues. Similar important differences in filtered and unfiltered questions are reported for the foreign policy questions examined by Lipset (1976).

Bishop et al. also drew different conclusions about the effect of filtering on the division of public opinion: One question they examined produced a 10 percentage point differential between the filtered and the unfiltered versions. Moreover, they found examples of some filtered questions that significantly increased correlations between attitude items, which is consistent with the expectation that people with less-structured opinions would be the ones filtered out, much as one would hope. However, in most cases, the two forms were not different in this respect—much as Schuman and Presser found.

In general, then, the results from these experiments are neither consistent nor systematic enough to provide firm guidance on the use of filtered questions in all circumstances. Some of the examples in chapter 4, however, argue for using the DK filter to describe opinion on certain issues—particularly those involving more obscure foreign policy issues. In the case of the SALT II polls in Tables 1 and 2, these filters provided documentation of the increasing proportions of the public who were willing to express an opinion as the issue was given increasing mass media attention in 1978. It is an unfortunate fact that on many issues of apparently vital concern, large segments of the public simply do not have an opinion. By not providing the convenient "out" of a filter, poll results create the misimpression that most people have thought about and developed opinions on an issue.

The misleading nature of unfiltered questions is illustrated by the very interesting experimental results obtained by both Schuman and Presser and Bishop and his associates. Each addressed the question of "non-attitudes" in the public by asking their respondents to express opinions on nonexistent issues (e.g., the Public Affairs Act) or virtually unknown issues (e.g., the Agricultural Trade Act). In both instances, almost a third of the respondents expressed an opinion when unfiltered questions were asked (versus less than 10 percent when the filter was provided). While it is

113

tempting to conclude that 20-25 percent of responses to unfiltered questions are meaningless, the more appropriate conclusion is that filters clearly reduce the possibility that unwarranted responses will affect the character of public opinion data.

Further research will be necessary to determine the conditions under which relations between variables are affected by using filtered questions. But for issues of foreign policy, filtered questions do seem to provide more accurate characterizations.

2. Middle Alternatives

In a separate set of experiments, Schuman and Presser generally obtained results that were similar to those obtained with the DK filter. In addition to the substantial numbers of respondents who may not have an opinion on an issue, there are many who have moderate rather than extreme attitudes on an issue; thus a third (or middle) alternative significantly increases the proportions who express this position.

Moreover, middle alternatives do not generally affect the pro-con division of opinion on an issue. Schuman and Presser found that provision of the middle option "did not alter the relationship between an item and a number of other respondent characteristics." [7] In a survey questioning attitudes on the amount of U.S. aid to Vietnam in 1974, Schuman and Presser found 15 percent of a national sample volunteered the response "right amount," 64 percent thought we provided "too much" aid and 10 percent "not enough" aid when those were the only options offered; 11 percent said "Don't know." However, when the "right amount" alternative was offered (to other respondents in the sample), it was chosen by 26 percent of the sample, an 11 percentage point increase.[8] When repeated in the 1978 national election study, much the same results were obtained with the proportion saying "right amount" increasing from 8 percent (when not explicitly offered) to 23 percent (when offered).

Schuman and Presser concluded that the decision to include or omit middle alternatives should be made on the basis of what the survey researcher wants to accomplish.

3. Balanced Alternatives

Here the research suggests that the pro-con divisions of public opinion *can* be affected by the form of the question. In 1951, Payne reported examples of up to 27 percentage point differences between balanced alternative and agree-disagree questions on the same topic.[9] More recently, in 1976, Lipset reported a difference of 26 points between a balanced alternative and an agree-disagree version of a question asked by the University of Michigan's Center for Political Studies and a 34 point spread on another question. At the same time, two other parallel questions in the study showed practically no difference across the two formats.[10]

Much the same lack of consistent results has occurred for controlled experimental studies of the two types of format. The largest difference was reported by Schuman and Presser in 1977: While 60 percent of respondents agreed (versus disagreed) that "individuals are more to blame than social condition for crime and lawlessness in this country," only 43 percent chose the "individuals" option in the balanced-alternative version of the question: "Which in your opinion is more responsible for crime and lawlessness in this country—social conditions or individuals?"[11] While this 17 percentage point difference was among the largest that Schuman and Presser found, it appears that distribution of public opinion was generally affected when only one side of the issue was presented to respondents in agree-disagree formats. Explicit presentation of both sides of the issue does sway opinion.

Thus it appears that pollsters would be better off with balanced alternative items than with agree-disagree items. As Schuman and Presser concluded in 1981, "Balanced questions rather than agree-disagree items are to be preferred . . . . "[12] Bishop et al. (1978) have provided (nonexperimental) evidence that the balanced alternative format generates higher correlations with other attitude items.[13]

4. Open and Closed Questions

Probably the oldest controversy in the literature related to the framing of questions concerns open-ended and closed-ended questions. Proponents of closed-ended questions point to their lower cost, greater efficiency, and minimal ambiguity which all have contributed to their greater popularity. Although they are rarely used, open-ended questions are favored for their ability to ferret out the meanings and frames of reference behind the public's views on issues and because they avoid the researcher-imposed constraint and bias of closed-ended questions. It is also argued that open-ended questions yield more consistent results. Nonetheless, open-ended questions do require careful and costly coding schemes to make them amenable to analysis.

Even though they were unable to provide evidence for the superiority of open-ended questions, Schuman and Presser argue that they should play a more prominent role in the polling process. They recommend, for example, that "important questions should be developed first by using an open question form in a sufficiently large poll study" in order to establish and understand the frames of reference that respondents bring to the issue.[14] They also note how rapid changes in events render many closed-ended questions obsolete. Open-ended material are thus more adaptable for long-range historical comparisons.

Pollsters need to determine whether the open-ended or closed-ended format is more appropriate for their goals. Neither is superior for all conditions; both have unique and independent value.

Context Effects

The effect of question context was researched by Turner

and Krauss in 1978 and their findings appear to contradict Sudman and Bradburn's more traditional conclusions from 1974 that "there do not appear to be any sizable response effects associated with the placement of questions." [15] Turner's research provides the strongest argument for taking context effects more seriously.[16] In some ways, the effects resemble those associated with providing information to respondents, since information also alters the context of the question. Further concern about context effects was voiced by Schuman and Presser in 1981. "Context effects are a serious hazard and any attempt to compare marginal results from one survey to another . . . . should avoid removing a single question from a context of related items."[17] They reached this conclusion despite the fact that several of their experiments showed minimal context effects. The problem, they argued, is that one never knows when one will encounter these differences due to context.

As an example of how context effects may affect foreign policy surveys, consider Lipset and Schneider's 1977 study of opinion on aid to Israel. They described a 1974 Yankelovich, Skelly and White question that produced only 31 percent support for military aid to Israel when it was presented in the context of aid to several countries. In this question, South Vietnam and South Korea (where U.S. aid was already substantial) preceded Israel on a list of proposed recipient countries. In contrast, four 1974-75 Harris questions revealed consistently firm support (63 percent to 68 percent) for such military aid; these were preceded by several questions establishing the likelihood of further Arab-Israeli conflict as the focus of the respondents' attention rather than military aid per se, as in the Yankelovich question. Lipset and Schneider concluded:

> Questions on "U.S. military aid to Israel" appear to involve two different signals: Americans have a strongly negative attitude toward *military aid* in general and a strongly positive attitude toward *Israel*. The response to any par-

ticular question will depend on the balance of emphasis between these two signals.[18]

Context effects are thus particularly important in "omnibus" polls that cover several widely different types of questions, and as we have seen, that is the context in which most foreign policy poll questions are asked.

6. Order Effects

Attention must be paid not only to the order of each question in a survey but to the order of alternatives and options within each question. Should one ask option A first or option B first? While most researchers have not found important differences in responses, in 1977 Schuman and Presser reported an important order effect in an experiment with two forms of an agree-disagree question. In one question format, respondents were asked to agree or disagree that "*individuals* were more to blame for crime and lawlessness in society than *social conditions*"; in the other format, the order was reversed with social conditions listed first. When individuals were listed first, 60 percent chose individuals. When social conditions were listed first, only 43 percent chose individuals. Here a 17 percentage point difference in public opinion appeared simply because the order of the two options was reversed.

More recently, Schuman and Presser found similarly important effects when balanced alternative questions with three response options were presented. In some cases, differences of more than 10 percentage points were found across the options "too much," "about right," and "too little" rather than "too much," "too little," and "about right." But in other cases, the order effect did not appear consistently or systematically, and the authors have no simple explanations for why the effect occurs in some situations but not in others.

7. Providing Information

Many polling agencies include background information

when introducing new or complex issues to respondents. As we saw in our analysis of polls on the Panama Canal, when Gallup included the information that "the United States would retain the right to defend the Canal," their poll showed greater support for the Treaty than other polls taken at the same time. In 1973, Mueller cited a Gallup study done during the Korean War that showed high anti-war sentiment when respondents were provided information that the Chinese military forces were far larger than U.S. forces. Lipset in 1976 noted that two similar questions concerning aid for Israel, each preceded with different background information, yielded strikingly different responses. He reported how in January 1975, Harris obtained a 66 percent positive response to aid for Israel when respondents were told:

> As you know, the United States has sent planes, tanks, artillery and other weapons to arm Israel. The Russians have sent similar military supplies for Egypt and Syria. In general, with the Russians arming Egypt and Syria, do you think the United States is right or wrong to send Israel the military supplies it needs?[19]

One month earlier, Yankelovich found that only 31 percent of the public agreed that the United States should sell arms to Israel:

> The United States sends arms and military equipment to a number of foreign countries. Do you personally feel the United States should or should not send arms to Israel (included on a list with other countries)?[20]

By including information that implied that Israel needed the arms to survive, the Harris question tilted responses in the pro-aid direction.

Given the extreme difficulty of avoiding biased information in statements designed to inform respondents, the more prudent approach would be simply to use a "Don't know" filter to eliminate or identify those who are uninformed rather than to try to instantly educate respondents. While it may be useful to learn how people would react *if* they were better informed, there must be a benchmark against which to measure opinion changes due to information given in the question. Thus if questions containing information are asked, there is the need to ask a non-informative version as well—either as a split ballot or as an introductory question.

8. Strength of Opinion

No experimental data exist on the relationship between asking respondents how strongly they feel about an issue and the overall direction of responses. Despite the great policy value in knowing how strongly people feel on an issue, including the "Strongly agree" or "Strongly disagree" options, finding this information is both time consuming and potentially confusing to respondents, particularly in telephone interviews when respondents have no nonverbal cues. One way to solve this problem is by attempting to ascertain intensity of opinion after respondents have expressed agreement or disagreement. But this is also time consuming if many questions are being asked. Perhaps the solution lies in using balanced alternative questions with a middle alternative. In this way, people with less strong opinions can choose the middle alternative, or the "No opinion" filter if that is also to be provided.

9. Aspects of Issues

Any social or political issue can be approached from several aspects and described to respondents in more than one way. In the case of East-West trade relations, for example, one could focus on the principle of trade with the Soviet Union, the type of products to be traded, the conditions of trade, or whether trade should be contingent on other Soviet policies.

A dramatic illustration of the problems arising from issue definition in the case of the Watergate crisis was described by poll critic Michael Wheeler in 1975. A series of 1974 Harris polls that portrayed the public as opposed to impeachment of President Nixon asked if they felt the president should be "impeached *and* removed from office." Polls conducted by Caddell, Roper, and Peter Hart, which did not mention removal from office, all found more support for impeachment than the Harris polls.[21]

As Table 5 in chapter 4 showed, distinctly different impressions emerged from questions about general support of the principle of detente than from questions about the beneficiaries of detente. In the same chapter we saw that President Carter received approval for "championing human rights" and standing up for the rights of Soviet dissidents but disapproval for "telling the Soviets how to treat their own citizens." The most dramatic divergence examined in chapter 4, however, occurred for polls on the SALT II Treaty that examined several different themes and aspects of that Treaty, such as Senate approval, the risk of treaties with the Soviet Union, or the general need for such agreements.

The limited research that has been done on issue definition suggests that pollsters have some obligation to the public to specify more clearly the many aspects of each issue under examination. While it would be impossible to catalog all the potential aspects of complex foreign policy questions, it seems useful to us to group the major approaches available to researchers of international issues. The following five categories seem to cover most of the poll questions we have examined.

1. Approval/disapproval of the general policy.
2. Approval/disapproval of the specific policy.
3. Benefits/value of the specific policy.
4. Policy change, or implementation of the specific policy.
5. Acceptance of the costs of the specific policy.

Thus in the case of the SALT II Treaty, questions dealing with the wisdom or importance of arms agreements with the Soviet Union would fall in the first category, while questions dealing with specific acceptance of a *new* arms agreement would fall in the second. The third category would include those questions dealing with how much the U.S. would gain from such an agreement or whether the Soviet Union would gain more than the U.S. The more specific question—whether the U.S. Senate should *ratify* this new treaty—falls into the fourth area, since it involves a change in existing policy or the implementation of new policies. Policy questions that seek to determine whether the U.S. should increase or decrease its efforts to achieve an arms agreement also fall in this category. Finally, we have encountered questions dealing with people's willingness to accept the possible costs of policy change. Would the public be willing, for example, to have their income taxes increased to implement the policy?

Even though each of these approaches has its advantages and value, we have encountered strong evidence in chapter 4 that these five aspects are unlikely to provide convergent results. Far more people said, for example, that the United Nations was not effective (category 3) than said we should not cooperate with it (category 1), and more people said that cooperation should be limited than said the U.S. should withdraw from the U.N. (category 4).

From our examination of poll questions, we would argue for the particular value of category 4 questions, if only one question can be asked or relied upon for analysis. It most directly addresses the concerns of the policy maker because it most clearly defines what policy the public would like to follow. The public may well approve or disapprove of a policy, but such opinions provide no specific guidance on what the public wants to see done or whether policy makers have taken too soft or too hard a stand on the issue. A properly phrased policy action question provides this guidance. Whenever possible, findings should be verified and refined through questions from different perspectives and through open-ended questions.

10. Wording

Although possibly the greatest variation in responses occurs in this area, research has provided little guidance for minimizing misunderstanding and misinterpretation. According to Schuman and Presser, "The alteration of one seemingly innocuous word may—though it may not—shift meaning in unintended ways. Thus every attempt to design experiments that deal with generic question forms flies in the face of the fact that every question is unique. . . . This may be the greatest obstacle of all."[22]

One of the studies on which they base this conclusion is their replication of Rugg's 1941 finding that the apparent antonyms "forbid" or "allow" yield different responses. Rugg had found that 21 percent in one random experimental group agreed that speeches "against democracy" should be "allowed" while some 39 percent in the other random group agreed that such speeches should "not be forbidden." Lipset and Schneider noted that pollsters registered different views of public opinion on American overseas troop commitments depending on whether Americans should be "willing to send troops" or should "refuse to get involved."[23]

Question wording also may affect one of the mainstays of polling—measures of presidential popularity. In 1977, Lipset and Schneider noted that Gallup and Harris may have obtained different readings of presidential popularity because Gallup asked simply whether people approved or disapproved of the way the president was handling his job, while Harris asked for ratings in one of four categories—excellent, pretty good, only fair, or poor.

Two sociologists, Lenski and Leggett, documented in 1960 how difficult it was to convey the same meaning when they attempted to write a "reversal" of a question tapping people's feelings about the future. They found that two-thirds of the respondents who agreed with the statement: "It's hardly fair to bring children into the world the way things look for the future," also agreed with the reversal they attempted to construct: "Children born today have a wonderful future to look forward to."[24]

In 1976, Lipset presented a particularly detailed and vivid illustration of how changes in question wording can affect the responses obtained. He described a survey experiment in which different random samples were interviewed about their confidence in various American institutions. The institutions were described in different words to different respondents. Respondents who were asked to rate the "Army, Navy, and Air Force" rated them much more favorably than respondents asked to rate "the military"; "established religion" was rated more highly than "organized religion"; and "business" and "labor" were rated more highly than "big business" and "big labor." There was some tendency for the institutions to rate higher than the people who lead them: Thus "the military" rated higher than "military leaders," "established religion" higher than "religious leaders" and even "organized labor" higher than "labor leaders."[25]

Many of the other examples we have considered in this chapter may also be considered to involve wording problems and ambiguities. Although there are many aspects of question wording to be considered, little solid research evidence is available for guidance. Among the problems that pollsters need to consider are:

1. The *time frame* of a question and the bearing this may have on responses. Using an immediate time frame may provide a "timely" reading of opinion but at the cost of minimizing historical value for detecting trends in public opinion.

2. The *abstract-concrete* dimension. Does one ask ques-

tions about improving relations with the Soviet Union in general or about the concrete policy of trade with the U.S.S.R.? Does one ask about human rights in general or about the Soviet treatment of dissidents in particular?

3. The *hypothetical-actual* distinction. This arises in interpreting and placing faith in answers to such questions as "Would you be willing to contribute money directly to people in the Third World?" or "Should we send troops to defend (some country) if it is attacked?"

4. The *precise terminology*. Does it matter if Eastern bloc countries are referred to as Communist or as Socialist, or if less-developed countries are described as poor, as developing, as underdeveloped, or as Third World nations?

5. Providing *context*. Should one contrast the conflicting goals of pressuring for human rights and making trade (or weapons) agreements with the Soviet Union, or examine them solely as separate issues? Unless such conflicts or trade-offs are mentioned in some questions, respondents may not be aware of them or think of them. (This is the reason for our support of the balanced alternative format.)

Even this is not an exhaustive list of dilemmas that confront the pollster who wishes to construct a fair and reasonable set of policy questions. Concerns about issues of question wording are shared by most experienced pollsters. George Gallup in his *Sophisticated Poll Watcher's Guide* stated that we can

> rest assured that the wording of every question is "agonized over." Nothing is as difficult, nor so important, as the selection and wording of questions. In fact, most of the time and effort of the writer [i.e., Gallup] in his work in this field has been devoted to this aspect of polling.[26]

Many years ago the Gallup organization developed a very promising question design format that it called the "quintamensional approach." It provided probes into five different aspects of opinion—awareness, overall opinion, reasons for views, views on specific aspects of an issue, and intensity. The first three of these aspects would be asked in an open-ended format to provide the types of respondent-generated information we see as most useful.

Gallup has described several interesting and sophisticated examples of question areas that can be examined with this approach. However, we have been unable to locate any examples of issues that have been illuminated by this approach since it was proposed. The "quintamensional approach" is clearly more expensive than the usual one or two closed-ended poll questions that are currently reported in the media, which may account for the failure of the firm to use this research format more widely.

Evaluating Foreign Policy Questions

Figure 3 provides a summary glimpse of the pattern of results from the various experimental studies that have been reviewed in this chapter. Clearly there is insufficient scientific evidence to support rigid judgments about how to frame and compose poll questions. But on the basis of the broad range of factors we have discussed and subject to the qualifications we have mentioned, we offer the following suggestions for pollsters interested in improving the results of their surveys.

We see greater value in using filtered questions and in providing specific middle (neutral or mixed) alternatives and in presenting policy options than in using a simple agree-disagree format. Nonetheless, we do recognize that the agree-disagree format usually does provide accurate portraits of the division of public opinion on an issue. Yet we still feel it is more instructive and appropriate to allow people to have the comfortable options of expressing "no opinion" or taking middle-of-the-road positions. Providing both sides of an issue explicitly to respondents in balanced alternative form has much the same salutary effect.

FIGURE 3

| | QUESTION WORDING | | | |
| ASPECT OF ITEM CONSTRUCTION | | | CRITERIA | |
	1. RELATION TO DISTRIBUTION OF OPINION	2. RELATION TO DEMOGRAPHIC VARIABLES	3. RELATION TO OTHER ATTITUDES (CONSISTENCY)	4. RELATION TO PRIOR DATA (TRENDS)
1. "Don't know" filters; or "No opinion" filters	Little effect (Schuman-Presser) Some effect (Bishop et al.)	Little effect (Schuman-Presser) Some effect (Bishop et al.)	No effect (Schuman-Presser) Increases effectiveness (Bishop et al.)	Very useful
2. Middle alternative vs. none	Affects popularity of middle but not balance of opinion (Schuman-Presser)	Related to education (Schuman-Presser)	?	?
3. Balanced alternative vs. agree-disagree	Some effect (5-10%) on popularity of items (Schuman-Presser)	Not related (Schuman-Presser)	Has effect on some groups (Schuman-Presser)	?
4. Open vs. closed question	Some effect on popularity; closed better (Schuman-Presser)	Related to education (Schuman-Presser)	?	?
5. Context effects	Appears to affect popularity (Turner-Krauss)	Better-educated more affected (Turner-Krauss)	?	Very important
6. Order of options in question	Some effect but not consistent or systematic (Schuman-Presser)	?	?	?
7. Providing information in question	Appears to affect popularity	?	?	?
8. Strength of opinion	Very useful	?	?	?
9. Aspect of issue	Clear effects	?	?	Some effect but not consistent or systematic
10. Specific wording	Clear effects	?	?	Some effect but not consistent or systematic

We also take the Schuman-Presser results as evidence of the value of open-ended questions that give insight into the reasons behind opinions. In the same way, we also recommend greater vigilance in examining for context effects, both in terms of preceding questions and in terms of the ways specific optional answers are provided to respondents.

We strongly advise against presenting information to respondents. It seems much more appropriate to use a filter or a middle alternative than to force respondents to express a definite pro or con opinion. These unfiltered or two-alternative questions tend to reinforce or create an image of a public far more involved in an issue than it may actually be. Moreover, the task of providing respondents with nonbiased information seems extremely difficult.

Respondents should be allowed to express the strength of their opinions, although this can be expensive and may more effectively be handled by providing a middle or neutral alternative, i.e., giving respondents three options—pro, con and neutral. Pollsters and poll readers should still realize that on most issues no single question can capture the full range of public opinion. Also not more than one of the five types of objectives we have identified should be addressed by a single question.

Finally, greater sensitivity is needed to avoid biased questions and loaded words. All relevant aspects of an issue should be examined. Political neutrality is no guarantee of freedom from bias, since bias may be just as likely to arise unconsciously.

Summary

We have reviewed ten major facets of the question-framing process. We have used the term *question framing* as the title of this chapter for an important reason: Framing emphasizes the subjective and idiosyncratic nature of the process rather than the usual implication that there is some correct set of rules or principles to follow. In a sense, all questions are biased depending on how they are "framed."

Our findings lead us to conclude that perhaps the major fault of poll questions is that they fail to give respondents sufficient opportunity to express less-committed opinions; not enough options are offered to people who have not developed a firm opinion or who endorse middle-of-the-road opinions. Efforts to inform respondents instantly in order to solicit an opinion places them under undue pressure and in unrealistic settings. All of this may spring from the overemphasis on reducing the "Don't know" responses.

This pressure on respondents to choose one of two options is perhaps also a consequence of the referendum scenario, i.e., the view that polls are a voting booth in which respondents *must* choose between only two candidates. Perhaps the newspaper editors who choose to publish polls with such frequency will see the folly of extending this scenario to issues, as many policy makers have already.

The issues in question wording touched on in this chapter do not exhaust the potential problems and pitfalls the survey researcher faces when constructing a questionnaire. Moreover, much of the evidence on the effects of question variation is mixed, and on some considerations the evidence is inconclusive. The tendency for analysts and journalists to hastily report changing trends "for" or "against" an issue without regard to subtleties of question wording, context, filtering, and so forth can lead to serious misjudgments of the state of public opinion. Although we have no firm solution to all the dilemmas confronting question framers, we hope that greater sensitivity to these issues will yield more meaningful and useful policy questions.

Notes

1. Samuel Stouffer et al., *Measurement and Prediction* (Princeton: Princeton University Press, 1950), p. 709.

2. Stanley Payne, *The Art of Asking Questions* (Princeton: Princeton University Press, 1951), p. 6.

3. Reliability generally refers to the ability of questions to produce *consistent* results—either across time or across respondents. That is the main criterion that has been investigated in the studies reviewed in this chapter. The validity of a question, which is usually tested by relating a question response to a person's behavior, has not been as systematically examined as a function of variation in question wording. Indeed it is hard to imagine realistic ways to test the validity of responses to questions on foreign policy because of the limited range of behaviors involved. The problem of validity, then, goes to the heart of a crucial aspect of public opinion research: the relationship between people's expressed opinions and their actual behavior.

4. Howard Schuman and Stanley Presser, "The Assessment of 'No Opinion' in Attitude Surveys," *Sociological Methodology, 1979*, p. 271.

5. Ibid.

6. Ibid. However, Schuman and Presser did note one instance in which a DK difference did drop to 10 percentage points.

7. Howard Schuman and Stanley Presser, "The Measurement of a Middle Position in Attitude Surveys," *Public Opinion Quarterly*, Spring 1980, p. 80.

8. The proportion saying "too much" dropped to 56 percent; "not enough," 8 percent; and "don't know," 9 percent. Thus the ratio of "too much" to "not enough" stayed at about the same ratio of 7-to-1.

9. Payne, *Art of Asking Questions*, pp. 7-8.

10. Lipset, "The Wavering Polls," p. 77.

11. Howard Schuman and Stanley Presser, "Question Wording as an Independent Variable in Survey Analysis," *Sociological Methods & Research*, November 1977, p. 158.

12. Schuman and Presser, *Questions and Answers*, p. 312.

13. The fairly standard practice of short-cut balancing—by inserting the word "disagree" or "oppose" into an item—seems to have little effect on the outcome. Whether one asks "Do you favor position X" or "Do you favor *or oppose* position X" makes little difference in proportional distributions of opinion, according to Schuman and Presser (1981).

14. Schuman and Presser, *Questions and Answers*, p. 312.

15. Seymour Sudman and Norman M. Bradburn, *Response Effects in Surveys: A Review and Synthesis* (Chicago: Aldine Publishing Co., 1974), p. 33.

16. Turner and Krauss (pp. 466-467) found that 53 percent of respondents said that their federal income taxes were "too high" (versus 40 percent "about right" and 1 percent "too low") when the question was preceded by a question describing several fair uses of tax money. When it was not preceded by such a question, 63 percent said that taxes were too high (versus 26 percent "about right" and 1 percent "too low"). In his more recent examination of survey questions in 1979, Turner found that up to 10 percentage point more married respondents described themselves as "very happy" when the question about their overall happiness followed a question about the happiness of their marriage. (Presumably the first question reminded respondents of marriage's major contribution to their overall happiness.) This result appears (Turner and Martin, *Surveys of Subjective Phenomena*, p. 29) along with the results of two other studies which did not replicate this direction of effect.

17. Schuman and Presser, *Questions and Answers*, p. 311.

18. Lipset and Schneider, "Polls for the White House," p. 32.

19. Lipset, "The Wavering Polls," p. 80.

20. Ibid.

21. Michael Wheeler, *Lies, Damn Lies and Statistics* (New York: Liveright Publishing Corp., 1975), pp. 6-10.

22. Schuman and Presser, *Questions and Answers,* p. 311.

23. Lipset and Schneider, "Polls for the White House," p. 30.

24. The Lenski and Leggett results were subsequently replicated by Fischer in 1973. Lenski and Leggett obviously failed to construct a perfect reversal. People apparently can see the future generation facing a world that is basically unfair but potentially highly promising. Lenski and Leggett's attempt illustrates the fate of researchers contemplating different ways of asking the same question, or asking about slightly separate aspects of the same issue. There is also the danger that simple changes in question wording may also change the aspect of the issue being examined.

25. Lipset further noted that these differences were not always reflected in responses at the other end of the scale; i.e., the proportions who express "no confidence" in these groups and leaders. Thus while 20 percent expressed a great deal of confidence in the "election polls" and only 14 percent in "public opinion pollsters," some 35 percent expressed *no* confidence in "election polls" and only 18 percent *no* confidence in pollsters; thus the term "election polls" elicited both more positive *and* more negative responses than did pollsters.

26. George H. Gallup, *The Sophisticated Poll Watcher's Guide* (Princeton: Princeton University Press, 1972), p. 77.

7 *Improving Issue Polls*

THROUGHOUT THIS BOOK we have documented certain disturbing divergences in poll results across a variety of foreign policy issues. One product of these divergences appears to be a new version of the "phantom public" that Walter Lippmann described almost a half century ago. This new version sometimes resembles a Janus-faced creature that supports opposite sides of the same issue depending on whose poll one reads.

We have also reviewed some research that we think accounts for many of the reasons for divergences. The words used in the questions, when carefully examined, offer one explanation. Several other facets of framing questions—question filters, the number of alternatives offered in closed-ended questions, the general context in which questions are presented—can affect results as well.

Divergent poll results are not without benefit. They can reveal the extent to which the public is troubled by subtle factors or ambiguities on an issue; to the extent that opinions are clear and strong, they will be unaffected by question wording differences. Poll divergences can also serve to prevent development of the "echo chamber" form of government that had concerned the noted political scholar V.O. Key.[1] Any tendency for a politician to expect poll data merely to echo his own position is precluded by findings that show the public to hold contrary views on the same issue.[2]

Yet, on balance, divergences in poll findings constitute a considerable problem, chiefly because they seriously limit the use of polls for policy making. Granted, some positive steps are being taken to address the problem, several of which we have noted. Within the U.S. Department of State and the Congressional Research Service, polls on policy issues are regularly reviewed, digested, and analyzed for trends.[3] In addition two recent Washington-based periodicals—*Public Opinion* magazine and the *Opinion Outlook* newsletter—regularly feature sophisticated analyses of poll data trends, often highlighting and explaining divergent poll results.

There is, moreover, the very promising line of academic research that has been undertaken at the University of California at Berkeley. Political researchers there are developing a sophisticated interviewing scheme to identify and help resolve the ambiguities of public opinion on complex issues, particularly those involving tradeoffs. Respondents are first asked to express their opinions on closed-ended questions on an issue. They are later confronted with the contradictions that naturally arise across these questions and are asked to think these inconsistencies through to a more considered final opinion.[4]

Encouragingly, pollsters themselves are developing more sophisticated techniques. Recent research by Yankelovich, Skelly and White is aimed at gauging the intensity and stability of public response. "We need to know," says Daniel Yankelovich, "when a figure citing '60 percent approval' means that 60 percent of the public has truly 'decided' in favor of a particular alternative or when '60 percent approval' means mere 'lip service.'"[5] His organization developed a "mushiness scale" to determine the degree to which a given issue affects a respondent. The less personal involvement and commitment a respondent's answers show, the more his/her "mushiness" rating rises. Preliminary results indicated that the public is "very mushy" on foreign policy issues, but only "somewhat mushy" on issues which touch both domestic and foreign policy. They remained firmest on domestic, social, and ideological issues.

Nevertheless, it's doubtful that the problems raised throughout this book can be dealt with adequately merely by the invention of more sophisticated techniques. Improved techniques alone will not offer a strong enough alternative to the "referendum scenario" to which the media, the pollster, and perhaps the policy maker have fallen prey. For more reliable and more comprehensive readings of public opinion, we need (1) more unstructured communications between the pollster and the polled; (2) a more informed exchange between polling organizations and those who try to interpret survey findings; and (3) perhaps above all, a stronger commitment to continuing experimentation in questionnaire design and polling procedures. Toward these ends, we offer the following recommendations:

1. Polling organizations should explain which aspects of an issue they have chosen to examine and how their treatment differs from similar investigations by other organizations. It would also be useful to know why the organization felt certain aspects of an issue were more important than others.

2. Polling organizations should explain what question-wording options were considered and why others were discarded in favor of the wording chosen.

3. On major pro-con issues, polling organizations should be encouraged to develop specific policy on whether or when they should:
   a) Use an explicit "Don't know" or "No opinion" filter.
   b) Use the balanced alternative (or forced choice) method to help respondents gain a better perspective on the issue.
   c) Provide a middle-of-the-road or neutral alter-

native for those who do not find either of these choices acceptable.

    d) Employ open-ended questions. Small pretests could be given to roughly representative samples or the "random probe" technique—where certain responses to closed-ended questions are followed by open-ended probes—could be employed.

4. Given the evidence that a little information can be misleading, attempts to instantly "inform" respondents with short descriptions of the situation should only be done with extreme care. Rather, respondents who have not thought about the issue should be encouraged to give "Don't know" or "No opinion" responses.

5. Far more questions need to be asked about the public's understanding of various foreign policy issues. Closed-ended information questions offer a great advance, but as indicators of public knowledge they can be as misleading as questions that require a simple pro-con choice.

6. We need further research into the connotations of specific words and phrases used in foreign policy polls.

Overall, we are suggesting that pollsters employ a more natural descriptive mode of polling instead of the typical referendum scenario. This mode would allow for larger proportions of the public to say (a) they simply have no opinion or they don't care about an issue or (b) they take a middle-of-the-road or moderate stand on the issue.[6] If pollsters want to see how these moderates or "don't knows" ultimately come down on an issue, this can be accomplished with a follow-up question. Put in more specific terms:

7. Rather than dividing respondents into the usual two groups, we suggest using at least four categories of opinion:

    a) Those with no opinion on the issue
    b) Those clearly pro
    c) Those clearly con
    d) Those in the middle or undecided
    This last group can be subdivided into two further categories: undecided but *leaning* pro and undecided but *leaning* con. We also suggest getting some comments from respondents in each of these groups in order to understand the rationale or frame of reference underlying their opinions.

8. Given the multiple problems with questions, we think it misleading for poll organizations to state results as accurate within the error attributable to sample size alone. We suggest instead that such statements highlight the very real possibilities of nonsampling errors. Statements such as "these results are accurate within five percentage points *when the question is asked in this way*" would highlight the frailties of question wording. Poll readers and users, however, also need to be sensitized to other sources of non-sampling error: the placement of questions in the questionnaire, the instructions given to interviewers, the variability across interviewers, and similar problems inherent in the interviewing process.

Finally, we believe further experimentation is essential. Given the enduring attraction of the closed-ended approach to most pollsters, as well as policy makers and media editors, we make this final recommendation even more strongly than any of the others. Indeed it supersedes them for it alone can show whether any of these recommendations stand the test of time. The low cost, simplicity, and elegance of the split-ballot technique can not only answer research questions that will lead to more understandable poll results, but the difference can supply entertaining material and paradoxes for news consumers as well. As

Stanley Payne, the author of the classic work on question wording, wrote thirty years ago:

> One last recommendation that I have already stated many times but which deserves the prominence of these final words is this: Controlled experiment is the surest way of making progress in our understanding of question wording. Never overlook an opportunity to employ the split-ballot technique.[7]

Opening Up the Polling Process

What can be done to improve the interpretation of poll results in the long run? Because no important policy question can be properly interpreted without knowing *why* respondents have chosen their answer, one goal is to "open up" the polling process and to emphasize its *communication* function between policy makers and their constituents. While closed-ended questions help clarify "where the public stands," they often fail to reveal *why* the public feels as it does about an issue.

For exploring this aspect of public opinion, pollsters will need to make more extensive use of the kinds of in-depth interviews used successfully by ethnographers, social anthropologists, and clinical psychologists. While we are encouraged by the use that some pollsters make of verbatim statements by respondents in their reports, we would like to see this practice extended more systematically. In particular, the sampling precision of the pollster can be wedded to the insights of the anthropologist to provide a form of "representative ethnography."

This need not entail large samples or great expense. In our 1976 Pittsburgh survey, for example, we conducted an in-depth survey using only forty respondents chosen entirely at random from the public for personal interviews in their homes (Robinson and Holm, 1977). While we hardly recommend samples of this size, it was encouraging to find that the aggregate responses were remarkably similar to those of a randomly chosen telephone sample of 300. These free-form responses revealed thinking behind respondents' opinions that remains instructive today. For example, answers to open-ended questions showed a deep-seated mistrust of the Soviet Union—comments that would help us understand an alleged "rapid turnaround" of opinion following the Soviet invasion of Afghanistan or the Soviet arms buildup.

Our open-ended interviews also showed that non-elites are often apologetic and embarrassed when talking about foreign affairs. People expressed their opinions with great reticence, and often prefaced them with "I'm not sure about this, but. . ." or "I could be wrong, but. . . ." Such uncertainty, undetectable in published results of mass opinion surveys, is every bit as important for the policy maker to know as the numerical division of opinion.

More intensive studies of single individuals have also been quite revealing. Political scientist Robert Lane's 1959 work provided insights into the political ideology of the "common man" that were unobtainable from large-scale data sets. In their earlier classic study of public opinion, Harvard social scientists M. Brewster Smith, Jerome Bruner, and Robert White convincingly demonstrated the power of the multidimensional, in-depth approach to the study of attitudes.

They studied only ten men, not many more than the number of senior researchers involved on the project. However, they scrutinized the men's opinions about Russia using a variety of methods—clinical interviews, projective tests, information and intelligence quizzes, direct challenges of opinions in "stress interviews," and the like.

The study showed the artificialities of translating a person's attitudes into a single quantitative score. People who might agree on a policy option or whose answers appeared at the same point on an attitude scale usually arrived at that position for quite different reasons and through different assumptions and patterns of conceptualization about the issue.

It was also clear, much as in our studies, that these ten men had not thought very deeply or consistently about the abstract political issues and concepts involved, even though they were intellectually far above average. With the exception of two men, all indicated that "Russia was not particularly salient" and their "time perspective was little more than a generalized optimism or pessimism."[8] The men used many "short cuts" to form opinions, often adopting opinions expressed by others. The researchers tried to trace personal opinions back to their roots in the mass media or from friends of the participants although this was a difficult, painstaking, and uncertain process.

Despite the appearance of ideological inconsistency, the men remained firm under pressure. Stress interviews—in which each respondent was grilled by a panel of Harvard experts about their attitude inconsistencies and lack of information—yielded very little shift of opinion. Whether this result indicates personal strength in the face of authority or simply reveals how stubborn people can be in the face of their own ignorance, it did suggest that people cared enough about opinions expressed in their own words to stand up for them under heavy attack.

It is not necessary, however, to mount such an elaborate project to gain significant advantages from the more open-ended approach to representing public opinion. Smith, Bruner, and White concluded that "the best method of getting richer material about a man's opinion was the rather naive and direct device of asking him to talk about those things that matter most to him. . . and then to direct him from general values to the specific topic under discussion."[9] Poll organizations which employ the "funnel technique" by asking general open-ended questions followed by more and more specific closed-ended questions follow the same strategy.

Surveyors of people can validate their results by making

sure they examine each issue from at least three perspectives, much as surveyors of land do.[10] They could explore the affective, the cognitive, and the behavioral components of each attitude by including questions that ask, in effect, "How do you *feel* about the issue?" "What do you *think* about it?" and "What are you prone to *do* about it?" Pollsters can gain additional insight by asking for response to changed conditions ("Would you support position X *even if. . . ?*"). They could achieve even greater perspective by examining opinion using closed-ended, partially open and fully open-ended questions.

The time has come, we believe, to go beyond the simple survey as we presently know it. After all, we can look at a thousand watches and know approximately what time it is. But if we want to know what makes them tick, we'll have to open a few and look inside.

Toward a Closer Dialogue Between Policy Makers and the Public

The previous suggestions are based on several assumptions, perhaps the most central one being that the communication function currently served by polls could be best achieved by that most useful and natural form of communication, direct face-to-face discussion. The more polls approximate this communication process, the better. But there are numerous difficulties involved in bringing the public and policy makers into face-to-face contact. Assuming that one can find small samples of the public who can be said to reflect the view of the larger public, and who would be willing to participate in discussion with policy makers, and assuming that policy makers would be willing to devote the time and effort to this form of dialogue, we still feel the communication process would be very difficult. Much of the conversation would probably be used by policy makers to instruct the public on the multiple demands and constraints of their job or the complex policy options that have already been discussed and considered. The policy maker might well find the public less articulate or informed on issues than the least sophisticated member of the policy maker's own staff.

What then can we offer as a workable approximation of this technique that would provide firsthand but undigested public opinion data to the policy maker? Videotaped group discussions conducted by a skilled leader or videotaped man-on-the-street interviews with a representative sample of people could be edited to highlight the main features of public opinion thinking on a particular issue. We see far more policy value in this use of new communication technology than in other technologies, such as interactive cable television. Despite its speed and efficiency, the questions that are asked of cable TV viewers are open to the same problems we have detailed at length in this book.

New technologies make mass participation in public opinion surveying simpler, but they suffer from severe sampling problems that restrict their value. Interactive cable television systems, such as the QUBE system in Columbus, Ohio, permit subscribers to view on their home screens presentations of issues and then to electronically transmit their choices on policy alternatives. The cost of subscriptions not only restricts the size of samples for such video referenda, it serves to limit these samples to community residents of relatively high socioeconomic status.[11]

Electronic politics has been tried in other communities, some of which have replicated electronically the classic town meeting. Despite the convenience of monitoring policy debate via television and responding by phone or cable, turnout and interest have been disappointing even for salient issues.

All the same, we still feel that the major impetus for improved poll results will come from policy makers' interest in more sophisticated readings of public opinion. And that brings us back to the striking gap in our knowledge of how poll data are actually used by policy makers. The chapter 3 quotes from our roundtable participants represent a needed start, but we need far more "third party" behavioral evidence to support these statements, e.g., the experiences of those who have access to libraries of poll data or the memoirs of presidential Cabinet members.[12]

It would help to know simply how often legislators are exposed to poll data or on what issues or legislation they have sought guidance from polls—as well as how and why they read poll results. The same questions need to be asked about the other elites in the policy process—government bureau officials, lobby groups, and reporters and editors for the mass media. To date, the evidence is too ambiguous to allow confident evaluation. On the one hand, our own research suggests that poll data on foreign affairs reach and materially affect the behavior of few policy influentials; to the degree that this situation prevails, polls figure only as a routine exercise in symbolic politics. On the other hand, instances have been widely publicized—the denouements to Vietnam and Watergate come immediately to mind—where polling emerges as the ultimate example of democratic theory in action. Clearly, the organic relationship of polling to political authority needs to be more researched and better understood.

Notes

1. V.O. Key, Jr., *The Responsible Electorate* (Cambridge: Harvard University Press, 1967).

2. Such appears to have been the case during the Vietnam War when the polls rightly reflected disapproval of administration policies, but were misinterpreted as evidence that the public wanted to withdraw from the conflict for reasons articulated by the antiwar movement. According to more detailed survey evidence, opposition to Vietnam policy was more likely to come from those who wanted to escalate the conflict than from those who wanted to withdraw from it (Robinson and Jacobsen, 1969). Open-ended poll questions, which were only asked near the end of the Vietnam conflict, indicated that only a small minority of the population

seemed bothered by the moral arguments against the war publicized by the antiwar movement (Schuman, 1973).

3. Concern over policy interpretation of statistical data has also been raised in connection with "hard" government data as well as these "soft" poll data. Speaking at a June 1979 meeting of the North American Conference of Labor Statistics, James Bannon, former executive director of the Federal Statistical System Reorganization Project said, "We have opened up the statistical process to the risk of dangerous political abuse at worst. . . . We must have statistical conventions, but they have to be set within a political convention *before* the fact [not]. . . after we take the census or survey." (*Monthly Labor Review* [August 1979]: 2.)

4. Merrill Shanks et al., "Citizen Reasoning about Public Issues and Policy Trade-Offs," mimeographed (Berkeley: Survey Research Center, University of California, 1980).

5. Quoted in *Opinion Outlook*, 6 April 1981, p. 1.

6. Baron quotes one top pollster as follows: "I don't think it is really our job to create opinion. If people want to take a neutral position, they should be able to do so" (Alan Baron, "The Slippery Art of Polls," *Politics Today*, Jan.-Feb. 1980, pp. 23-24). Similarly, in his extensive critique of the polling profession, Leo Bogart concluded: "The first thing a pollster should ask is "Have you thought about this at all? Do you *have* an opinion?" (Bogart, "No Opinion, Don't Know and Maybe No Answer," *Public Opinion Quarterly 31* (1967): 337).

7. Payne, *Art of Asking Questions*, p. 237.

8. M. Brewster Smith, Jerome S. Bruner, and Robert W. White, *Opinions and Personality* (New York: John Wiley and Sons, 1956), p. 246.

9. Ibid., p. 286.

10. Some social scientists have adopted the term "triangulation" from land surveying to describe the process of achieving valid measurement by examining problems from three different perspectives.

11. In a recent instance, QUBE viewers were asked if they would be willing to pay a few cents more for products in containers with labels providing additional consumer information. The response was overwhelming in favor of the new packaging. With little consideration of their limitations these data were considered by officials at the Federal Trade Commission as an invitation to investigate the possibilities of introducing such packaging. Not only would those currently excluded from the QUBE system—mainly those least able to pay—have to bear the same cost as the more affluent subscribers to QUBE, there is no evidence to suggest that when confronted with an actual behavior choice—spend a few cents more or not when the two packages are sitting on the grocery shelf—that expressed preference would be translated into behavior.

12. One such person with access to poll data reported that most calls from policy makers were of the nature, "Do you have any polls showing support for policy X?" One troubling but honest response to public opinion data on an issue came from a member of parliament in a European country: "If I want that kind of information, I can talk to my cleaning lady."

Appendixes

A The Ten-City Study: Survey Methods and Questions

Prior to each of the "town meetings," 300 persons were interviewed by telephone. Each survey was commissioned by the Charles F. Kettering Foundation and was developed and supervised by the Communication Research Center of Cleveland State University. The sample in each city was drawn by a variant of the random digit dial method, which ensures that all telephone households in the city have an equal chance of selection—including unlisted numbers.

The specific survey questions used in the five cities sampled in 1977 and the responses to them are listed in the remainder of this appendix. The 1976 data are published in a separate report available from the Kettering Foundation.

Particular care was taken to avoid "agree-disagree" questions because they tend to push respondents to simply agree with a question, regardless of content. Instead, maximum reliance was placed on "forced-choice" or "balanced alternative" question formats, in which options are clearly presented to respondents.

In the following figures, the survey questions do not appear in the order presented to respondents.

FIGURE A.1
BASIC ATTITUDES AND PRIORITIES

1. First, do you *agree* or do you *disagree* with the following statements?

	Agree	Mixed	Dis-agree	DK*
a. The U.S. would be better off if we stayed home and did not concern ourselves with problems in other parts of the world	28%	8%	61%	3%
b. The U.S. cannot trust the Russians to live up to their agreements	63%	7%	22%	8%
c. This country's leaders really don't want to know what people like me think about foreign policy	52%	7%	35%	6%

*Don't know

2. Next, we have a list of possible things this country should *try to do*. For example, stopping the spread of dictatorships. Do you think this is *very* important, or only *somewhat* important, or *not* important for this country to *try to do* in foreign policy?

	Percent Responding "Very Important"
a. Protecting the jobs of American workers	85%
b. Influencing other countries to make agreements to prevent wars	82%
c. Making agreements with Russia to control nuclear weapons	75%
d. Stopping the spread of communism	67%
e. Giving food to countries where people don't have enough to eat	62%
f. Making sure the U.S. is the most powerful country in the world	60%
g. Reducing the sale of U.S. military equipment to other countries	52%
h. Speaking up when another country	

	Percent Responding "Very Important"
violates the human rights of its citizens	52%
i. Encouraging business and trade with other countries	52%
j. Stopping the spread of dictatorships	49%
k. Helping to raise the standard of living in less-developed countries	44%
l. Promote racial equality in South Africa	39%

FIGURE A.2

EAST-WEST RELATIONS

3. Do you think the U.S. military and defense budget should be *increased* or *decreased*, or *kept about the same* as it is now?

30%	47%	15%	8%
Increased	Same	Decreased	DK

4. How do you think U.S. military power *should* compare with that of Russia—should the U.S. spend whatever is necessary to *keep ahead* of Russia, should we *keep even* with Russia in military power or is it all right if the *U.S. gets slightly behind* Russia?

48%	42%	8%	2%
Keep ahead	Keep even	U.S. slightly behind	DK

5. At the present time, do you believe the U.S. is *ahead* of Russia in military strength, *about even*, or is the U.S. *behind* Russia in military strength?

18%	35%	33%	14%
Ahead	About even	Behind	DK

6. In recent years, the U.S. has been trying to improve relations with Russia. Do you think this effort has been a *good thing* or a *bad thing* for the U.S.?

73%	12%	11%	4%
Good	Bad	Mixed	DK

7. How would you describe relations between Russia and Mainland China at the present time—do you think their relations are *good, fair,* or *poor*?

9%	39%	40%	12%
Good	Fair	Poor	DK

8. Should the U.S. try to improve relations more with Russia, more with China or both about equally?

5%	9%	77%	5%	4%
Russia	China	Both equally	Neither	DK

FIGURE A.3

HUMAN RIGHTS

9. Do you think U.S. leaders should criticize countries that violate the human rights of its citizens or that it's none of our business to criticize what goes on inside another country?

48%	38%	5%	9%
Should criticize	None of our business	DK	Other

10. a. What about Russia? Do you think U.S. leaders should criticize Russia for violating the human rights of its citizens or that it's none of our business to criticize what goes on inside Russia?

47%	5%	43%	5%
Should criticize	Both	None of our business	DK

b. Do you think U.S. leaders should also criticize Russia for not having our kind of democratic government with competing political parties or do you think it's better not to make an issue out of it?

6%	4%	36%	1%
Should criticize	Mixed	Don't make issue	DK

11. Which one of the following three goals is most important for the U.S. in dealing with the Russians?

15% (a) Improving the human rights of Russian citizens
11% (b) Increasing trade with the Russians
71% (c) Working out an agreement to control the use of nuclear weapons

12. The U.S. should refuse to do business with any country that violates the human rights of its citizens, even if this country loses a lot of business doing it.

60%	22%	18%
Agree	Disagree	DK

FIGURE A.4

BUSINESS AND TRADE

13. First, do you *agree* or *disagree* with the following statements?

	Agree	Mixed	Dis-agree	DK

a. Except for oil, our economy would not be hurt very much if we stopped doing business with

151

	Agree	Mixed	Dis-agree	DK
other countries	27%	2%	66%	5%

b. The U.S. should keep a foreign product out of this country, for example TV sets, even if we have to pay more for the American product if this saves the jobs of American workers — 48% 4% 42% 6%

14. Some foreign companies want to build factories in the United States. Should the U.S. try to make it easy for such companies to build, make it hard for such companies to build, or what?

26%	29%	39%	6%
Easy	In between, depends	Hard	DK

FIGURE A.5

ARMS SALES

15. The U.S. sells arms and weapons to foreign countries. Do you think the amount of arms and weapons the U.S. is selling to other countries is *too much, about the right amount,* or *not enough*?

50%	22%	2%	26%
Too much	About right	Not enough	DK

16. Some people feel we should not sell arms and weapons to other countries under any conditions while other people feel that we should sell arms and weapons under some conditions. Which is closest to your own view?

30%	16%	49%	5%
Should not sell	Depends	Should sell	DK

a. Should we refuse to sell even if we know they will go out and buy the weapons from some other country?

23%	5%	2%
Yes	No	DK

b. Should we sell weapons to any other country that can pay for them?

14%	46%	5%
Yes	No	DK

FIGURE A.6

AID AND DEVELOPMENT

17. Some countries in the world are so poor that most of their people don't have enough food and clothing to keep healthy. Experts call these countries less developed. Do you think the U.S. should help less developed countries improve their standard of living or just let less developed countries solve their economic problems on their own?

57%	23%	4%	16%
U.S.	Own	DK	Depends

18. Here are different reasons that have been suggested either for giving or for not giving U.S. aid to less developed countries. Please tell me whether you *agree* or *disagree*.

	Agree
a. Aid from the U.S. will help to stop the spread of communism to less developed countries	44%
b. U.S. aid will promote their economic development so less developed countries will become able to take care of themselves	71%
c. Aid from the U.S. can help less devel-	

	Agree
oped countries avoid revolutions and uprisings	37%
d. It is our moral responsibility to feed starving people wherever they may be in the world	63%
e. The wrong people in a country always seem to wind up getting most of the U.S. foreign aid	63%
f. Less developed countries don't know how to use our aid wisely—they waste most of it	59%
g. Foreign aid hurts the American economy	35%
h. Any country can build itself up without outside help	23%

19. Many poor countries claim that the United States has not paid a fair price for *their* raw materials, like metal, oil, and coffee. Would you agree or disagree with this point of view?

21%	64%	15%
Agree	Disagree	DK

B Relation of Opinions to Personal Background Factors

This appendix examines certain background factors that can determine the accuracy of public opinion. These background factors identify important *sub*publics—the old or young, better educated or less educated, men or women, Republican or Democrat, and black or white. In several instances, we shall see important differences of opinion between these groups.

To facilitate this examination, the relations between background factors and opinion are presented in terms of an index called the correlation coefficient. This index shows, for example, the extent of agreement between the young and old on isolationism or between more- and less-educated people on human rights.

The correlation coefficient can be any value between 0.00 and 1.00. A .00 correlation indicates that variations of a particular background factor—such as age—show no difference of opinion on a given issue—such as isolationism. Hence a .00 correlation between age and isolationism means that older and younger people agree about isolationism. A 1.00 correlation coefficient, on the other hand, indicates perfect (100 percent) agreement: In the case of age and isolationism, if, for example, 100 percent of older people are isolationist, and no (0 percent) younger people are isolationist. Values of the coefficient between .00 and 1.00 indicate varying degrees of this strength of relationship. Values below .10 between two variables suggest a level of agreement beyond what would be expected solely on the basis of chancc, givcn the more than 1,500 people sampled in our 1977 survey. Values approaching .20 or above indicate a level of agreement that is also well beyond chance.

The correlation coefficients shown in Table B.1—called beta values—are different from other coefficients. Betas indicate the strength of relationships, taking other factors into account. In the case of foreign policy attitudes, for example, better-educated people and younger people tend to share the same (here less-isolationist) attitudes. But it is also the case that younger people are more likely to have had a college education.

Are younger people less isolationist simply because they have more education than older people? Or are better-educated people less isolationist because they are younger? In order to address this problem, we employed a technique developed for the analysis of social science data that allows several factors to be taken into account. In Table B.1, these factors are education, age, party identification, sex, and race. The computer program that generated these beta figures is called Multiple Classification Analysis and was developed by Andrews, Morgan and Sonquist (1969) for analysis of multivariate survey data. For readers more familiar with quantitative methods, it is a form of dummy-variable regression.

TABLE B.1

RELATIONS BETWEEN BACKGROUND FACTORS AND ATTITUDES, 1977 SURVEY

Position	Education	Age	Party	Sex	Race
	Values of *Beta** from Multiple Classification Analysis				
East-West Relations					
U.S. cannot trust Russians	.06*	.18*	.09	.07	.01
Stop communism—very important	.16	.03	.06	.10	.02
Make agreements—very important	.08	.02	.08	.01	.14
U.S. should be ahead	.19	.12	.13	.02	.09

	Education	Age	Party	Sex	Race
Position	Values of *Beta** from Multiple Classification Analysis				
U.S. is ahead	.03	.14	.06	.08	.02
U.S.-Soviet relations	.06	.10	.07	.03	.05
Increase military budget	.06	.04	.12	.08	.06
Third World					
Help less-developed countries (LDCs) develop—very important	.06	.08	.05	.02	.01
Give food to hungry—very important	.08	.03	.05	.05	.06
Help LDCs	.08	.09	.02	.05	.05
Communism	.09	.09	.09	.02	.01
Raises standards	.03	.08	.04	.02	.03
Stops revolutions	.08	.04	.05	.05	.08
Moral responsibility	.03	.04	.03	.05	.09
Wrong people	.13	.09	.04	.13	.61
Aid wasted	.14	.11	.02	.15	.04
Hurts economy	.13	.02	.06	.08	.05
Countries OK without	.12	.08	.02	.02	.01
Human Rights					
Criticize rights violators	.17	.12	.04	.02	.08
Criticize Russians on human rights	.20	.09	.04	.02	.07
No business with violators	.08	.02	.06	.07	.03
Stop dictatorships—very important	.10	.03	.09	.07	.00
Speak out on rights—very important	.06	.12	.09	.07	.00
Isolationism and Related Questions					
U.S. better stay home	.20	.07	.05	.03	.09
U.S. can go it alone economically	.11	.10	.02	.03	.08
Keep foreign products out	.16	.09	.04	.12	.08
Build foreign plants here	.17	.02	.02	.09	.07
Arms sales too much	.03	.10	.05	.07	.03
Sell arms to others	.07	.03	.05	.04	.05
Protect jobs—very important	.19	.06	.03	.08	.06
U.S. most powerful—very important	.14	.20	.05	.03	.08
Foreign trade—very important	.21	.09	.04	.07	.11
Prevent war—very important	.07	.02	.01	.07	.04
Reduce arms sales—very important	.02	.05	.04	.06	.02

*Like other correlation coefficients, values of beta vary between .00 (indicating no correlation) and 1.00 (indicating perfect correlation). Unlike most other correlation coefficients, beta does not take on positive or negative signs to indicate the *direction* of correlation. That is, the same value of beta is obtained if the particular attitude *increases* for each level of education or *decreases* with each level of education. We have often indicated the direction of correlation in the text.

In our analysis, we concentrated on values of beta that exceed .10. The most dramatic differences are also illustrated by simpler percentages in Table B.2.

East-West Relations: The most significant differences in opinions are found by age and by education. Older people distrusted the Soviet Union more than younger people and were more concerned about keeping the U.S. ahead of the U.S.S.R. militarily. Much the same age differences had been found in the 1976 surveys as well.

The 1976 surveys also identified education as having less effect than age on East-West attitudes, and one can see in Table B.1 that the less educated considered stopping the spread of communism to be a much more important goal than the better educated, a question on which no significant age difference was found. Table B.1 also shows the less educated to be more concerned about being ahead of the Soviet Union militarily than the better educated, although no education difference was found for the question on how this military balance was working out. These data suggest that the less educated were much more likely to feel that the Soviet Union had greater power than the United States.

Political party identification, a factor not examined in the 1976 surveys, was also a major predictor. Here the Independents expressed considerably more anti-Soviet feeling than Democrats or Republicans, particularly in terms of military preparedness; the Republicans, however, most favored increasing the military budget.

Differences by sex and race were not pronounced. Women were a little more likely than men to see stopping communism as an important goal, and blacks were more likely than whites to feel we should be ahead of the Soviet Union militarily and to see nuclear agreements with the Soviets as less important, but again those differences were not large.

Third World: As was true in the 1976 study (and many other national surveys), younger and better-educated respondents were more supportive of aid. However, in our survey these relations were not strong.

We found more pronounced differences in the justifications for giving or not giving aid to Third World countries. Better-educated respondents, and to a lesser extent younger respondents, were more likely to reject several arguments (as justifications) for not giving aid—that the aid was wasted, reached the wrong people, hurt our economy, and was not necessary for development.

Differences in Third World attitudes by party, sex, and race were generally minimal. Women, however, were significantly more likely to reject misdirected and wasted aid as a justification for not giving it to Third World countries.

Human Rights: The better educated were significantly more supportive of the government policy of criticizing human rights violators than were the less educated, not only in general but in the specific case of the Soviet Union. At the same time, they were *less* likely to agree that the U.S. should not do business with human rights violators or that stopping the spread of dictatorships was a very important goal.

To some extent these views were reflected by age as well. However, the relation to age was not regular or "linear": Oldest respondents (over age fifty) were least supportive of our government's human rights criticisms; the middle-aged were more supportive; while the youngest adults (between eighteen and thirty) fell in the middle.

Differences by party, sex, and race again were not large, although Democrats tended to see stopping dictatorships as more important and to favor cessation of business with human rights violators; but Democrats did not support criticizing violators any more than Republicans or Independents did.

Isolationism: Education was a major predictor of general isolationist attitudes. Better-educated people were less likely to feel that the U.S. could "go it alone" economically, to feel we should "buy American" even at greater cost, and to rate highly the goals of protecting American jobs, keeping America as the most powerful country in the world, and discouraging foreign trade.

Again these views of the better educated are also shared by younger people. (It will be remembered that the effects of age have been corrected for educational differences in the computer analysis.) As was true for general isolationism in chapter 5, the relation with age was not linear: On both items dealing with economic independence and keeping foreign products out of the country, the views of youngest and middle-aged respondents were virtually identical. On the importance of keeping the U.S. most powerful and encouraging trade, as well as feeling that arms sales were "too much," the youngest age groups were more "liberal" than the middle-aged.

While differences by political party were minimal, some interesting differences by race and by sex were found. Blacks and women tended to espouse more isolationist attitudes than did whites or men. (Again the differences by race have been adjusted for educational differences between blacks and whites.) It will be remembered that lower-income individuals were also found to be more isolationist in the 1976 surveys.

Thus, age and education emerged as the most important factors in the preceding analysis. These are examined more closely in Table B.2. Each entry shows the percent of each age-by-education subdivision of the population who agreed with the given (paraphrased) statement. For example, 60 percent of the eighteen to twenty-nine year-olds without a high school degree felt that we could not trust the U.S.S.R. compared to 74 percent of the thirty to forty-nine year-olds without a high school degree and 82 percent of those without a high school degree aged fifty and older. This 22 point differential between the eighteen to twenty-nine year-old group and the age fifty-plus group for those who had not completed high school increases to 28 points (75 to 47 percent) for those with a high school degree and to 30 points (80 to 50 percent) for those with at least some college education. These differentials generated the .18 beta value in Table B.1 for age on attitudes about trusting the Russians. The much smaller (and less regular) differences by education led to only a .06 value of beta for the relation between education and trust in the Soviet Union.

TABLE B.2

	SUPPORT FOR SELECTED QUESTIONS								
EDUCATION	HIGH SCHOOL INCOMPLETE			HIGH SCHOOL GRAD			COLLEGE		
AGE	18-29	30-49	50+	18-29	30-49	50+	18-29	30-49	50+
Position	*Percentage Indicating Agreement*								
East-West									
Cannot trust Russians	60%	74%	82%	47%	68%	75%	50%	59%	80%
Should be ahead of Russia	46	61	60	30	42	54	25	35	45
Stop communism important	75	80	81	58	45	66	43	46	64
Third World									
Should help less-developed countries	62	57	55	62	60	54	75	74	53
Aid wasted	64	79	88	50	73	68	53	58	65
Human Rights									
Criticize rights violators	46	48	35	58	59	34	74	69	55
Stop dictatorship important	57	61	63	42	50	45	40	28	36
Isolationism and Related Questions									
U.S. stays home	35	37	47	17	25	22	18	11	21
U.S. power important	49	72	81	30	54	64	81	64	61
Protect jobs important	92	94	93	86	86	87	75	63	64
U.S. leaders don't care	57	61	70	43	53	50	37	37	42

Another question showing a predominantly age effect (beta equals .09) concerned helping less-developed countries. Table B.2 shows this age difference to be mainly concentrated among the college educated. Likewise, differences by education are also evident, although not among those aged fifty and older.

Other questions also show combined age and education effects. These include keeping ahead of the Soviet Union militarily, feeling that because aid is wasted we should not give it, feeling that the U.S. government should criticize governments that violate human rights, and keeping the U.S. the most powerful nation. For each question area, younger and less-educated respondents tend to hold attitudes that resemble those of older and better-educated respondents. Such a pattern is most evident for the items dealing with keeping ahead of the Soviet Union and with concern over wasted foreign aid. In the former case, 46 percent of the eighteen to twenty-nine year-old group without high school diplomas said we should keep ahead of the Soviet Union; virtually the same figure, namely 45 percent, was found among college graduates over age fifty.

As in Table B.1, however, the effects of age differences tend to be relatively smaller than the effects of education differences. This can be seen as the basic pattern in five questions: feeling that the U.S. would be better off staying home, and that stopping communism, stopping dictatorships, and keeping the U.S. most powerful are important foreign policy goals for the country. The same pattern characterized responses to the domestic question of whether U.S. leaders care about the public's views; only in the group with the least education did older adults feel more than younger adults that leaders don't care.

If these patterns continue, then, one can expect a shift towards the liberal or less hard-line direction in the years ahead as the elderly die. These data suggest that such structural shifts (assuming no dramatic changes in the foreign affairs climate) are more likely to occur, however, as more people receive more formal education. Nonetheless, the future of public opinion will be shaped most dramatically by future events.

C Workshop Differences in Cleveland

In the 1977 town meeting in Cleveland, the usual plenary session was broken into four workshops, each on a special topic. We wanted to see how groups with a particular interest in one area would respond to all our questions and compare the responses of the four groups. Many of the workshop differences are predictable, but some are not.

The *East-West* group's views are most understandable, the group being decidedly anti-Soviet in orientation: 64 percent felt we should keep ahead of the Soviet Union militarily, more than twice as many as for any other group at the meeting. The East-West group also took a "hard-line" stand on other issues as well: anti-aid, pro-American jobs and arms sales, and, as noted at the bottom of Table C.1, more sympathetic to South Africa as well.

The *Human Rights* workshop did attract participants who thought the problem more important and who felt more willing to criticize the Soviet Union for human rights violations. But they were no more likely to agree to refusing to do business with human rights violators, nor to rate promoting democracy abroad and stopping dictatorships as important goals; and they were not much less sympathetic toward South Africa than the rest of the sample.

Anti-South Africa views *were* most likely to be expressed by participants in the *Third World* workshop, in which participants also attached more importance to the foreign

164

policy goals of stopping dictatorships and promoting democracy abroad. The Third World workshop members did not support foreign aid more than other workshops, nor the view that Third World countries were exploited economically. Less than half of the members of this workshop rated protecting the jobs of American workers as very important, far lower than any other group sampled.

Perhaps the most surprising results, however, are those for the workshop on the *Middle East*. It was a group that did not favor activist policies, neither keeping ahead of the Soviet Union militarily, criticizing the Soviet Union for human rights violations, nor promoting democracy abroad; it was also relatively high on isolationism. Most surprisingly, the group was neither more critical nor more approving than the other groups of Israel's policies in the Middle East.

TABLE C.1

ATTITUDES OF CLEVELAND WORKSHOP PARTICIPANTS

	TOWN MEETING WORKSHOPS				
	East-West	Third World	Human Rights	Mid-East	Total
Position	*Percentage Indicating Agreement*				
East-West Relations					
U.S. cannot trust Russians	76%	58%	60%	53%	59%
U.S. keep well ahead of Russia militarily	64	13	28	13	34
Favor U.S.-Russia agreements on nuclear power	38	56	70	75	62
Criticize Russia on human rights	79	60	74	44	66
Third World Relations					
U.S. should help less-developed countries (LDCs)	52	67	77	76	60
U.S. has not paid fair price for LDC raw materials	21	60	47	63	46
Intervention					
U.S. better off by staying home (agree)	0	0	10	17	6
U.S. arms sales too much	48	86	90	83	77
Make it easy for foreign countries to build in U.S.	32	50	14	38	34
Values					
Protect American jobs	70	31	66	50	54

	TOWN MEETING WORKSHOPS				
	East-West	Third World	Human Rights	Mid-East	Total
Position	*Percentage Indicating Agreement*				
Help LDCs	88	88	89	79	88
Persuade other countries to be democratic	44	64	48	35	49
Stop the spread of dictatorships	42	62	39	39	42
Stop the spread of communism	52	36	43	33	41
Speak up on human rights	50	40	83	50	57
Promote equality in South Africa	26	55	63	59	50
Encourage foreign business and trade	63	69	65	59	65
Human Rights					
Refuse business with human rights violators	23	57	58	56	46
Support UN condemnation of South Africa	63	90	73	73	75
Refuse arms sales to South Africa	61	91	84	77	79
Refuse trade with South Africa	26	50	57	38	42

Table C.1 contains several ambiguities and surprises that need to be examined further in subsequent research on the attitudes of people who attend multipurpose community meetings such as these. If gathered in advance of the formal proceedings, this information could well be used to identify areas of disagreement and thus sharpen the debate between workshop members.

Factor Analysis

In each of the cities studied in 1977, a clear structure of interrelationships between attitudes on the diversity of questions asked was identified by factor analysis. This multivariate procedure is designed to discover the most cohesive underlying dimensions (or *factors*) that unite a group of questions around a single issue. The analysis suggested that a set of eight meaningful factors existed in our data. The major factor in the forty-odd questions used in our 1977 polls was related to isolationism. Responses contributing to this factor consisted not only of those on the basic isolationism questions, but of those dealing with abandoning foreign trade, buying American products to save American jobs, discouraging foreign business, and making it hard for foreign countries to build in the United States.[1] The final component of the isolationism factor concerned refusing to do business with human rights violators, indicating that this item related more to people's feelings about foreign trade than to attitudes about human rights.

The second factor identified in this analysis connected items dealing with helping the countries of the Third World. The items included rating world hunger and helping less-developed countries as very important, feeling we should give aid to help such countries in general, and agreeing that it was our moral responsibility to help these countries. Two of the reasons for *not* giving aid (because it is wasted and misdirected) are less important aspects of this factor on the negative side of this dimension.

The third factor related items dealing with U.S. power in the world—making sure of U.S. superiority, increasing our military budget, and keeping well ahead of the Soviets militarily. Items dealing with the untrustworthiness of the Soviet Union and stopping the spread of communism were also related, but less strongly. Thus this factor suggests that respondents had the Soviet Union in mind when considering international power relations.

The five remaining factors each consisted of fewer items and appear less important. One of these related our three questions on arms sales, a second related the two questions on agreements limiting nuclear arms, and a third related three of the four reasons *for* giving aid. One of the final two factors related three (out of five) questions on human rights and the other related stopping communism and stopping dictatorships. Interestingly, these last two dimensions emerged independently of each other, meaning that human rights attitudes were only minimally related to the goal of stopping the spread of dictatorships.[2] This suggests that when our respondents referred to dictatorships, they meant communist dictatorships rather than other dictatorships that violated the human rights of their citizens. This reinforces the point we made earlier about the multiple and ambiguous meanings of the term "human rights."

Thus, the eight separate factors in our data identified by factor analysis are a diverse lot. They are so diverse that it would be unwise for foreign policy makers to expect that the public's attitudes on one issue will relate or be much affected by attitudes on another issue—no matter how logically they connect in the policy makers' minds. In other words, a person who opposes government policy on human rights may be no more or less likely to oppose it on another issue such as foreign aid. Likewise, people who take a "hard-line" position on one issue may not be inclined necessarily to be equally rigid on another.

At the same time, some experimental studies indicate that our usual two-alternative question format may have underestimated the degree of correlation or cohesion between issue areas. Nonetheless, many of the eight factors do include items employing different formats. This gives us somewhat more confidence that the identified factors are genuine ones.

The general nature of these factors is supported by a factor analysis that was performed on the data from a 1974 national study conducted by the Chicago Council (Bardes and Oldendick, 1978). This analysis identified five separate factors (each having more than five questions) from the far larger number of questions asked in that study. The first factor from this analysis of the Chicago Council data— "militarism"—connected a very similar set of questions to those located on our (third) factor concerning U.S. power. Their second and third factors—"involvement" and "world problems"—contained items that resembled many of those on our first and second factors (dealing with isolationism and helping Third World countries). Their fourth and fifth factors—"detente" and "international organization"—were not related to any of our remaining factors, but this may be because of the lack of further common items in the two studies rather than to differences in the underlying patterns that connect attitudes. Bardes and Oldendick also note the similarity of these factors to those found by other researchers—factors such as interventionism, isolationism, escalation, and hostility.

Finally, the correlations between these factors and personal background characteristics bear a strong resemblance to the findings in Appendix B for our data. Age and education in our data related strongly to the first two factors in the Bardes and Oldendick study, with better-educated and younger respondents supporting less-militaristic and more nonisolationist sentiments in these policy areas. Only insignificant differences were found by sex and race. Except for the attitudes of Independents toward the military, political partisanship was not significantly related to these factors. And the major difference across income groups was for the factor of isolationism (corresponding to our finding on the issue).

Notes

1. For readers familiar with factor analysis, all of these questions had factor "loadings" of over .30 on the rotated factor matrix initial factor.

2. This low correlation (r=.04) between the general questions on human rights and the importance attached to stopping the spread of dictatorships indicates that respondents who felt stopping the spread of dictatorships was an important policy goal were no more likely to support criticizing human rights violations in other countries than were respondents who saw it as a less important policy goal.

There are plausible post hoc reasons for this lack of relationship. The term *dictatorship* refers to only one human rights concern, although a fairly general one, and dictatorships do not necessarily engage in suppression of freedom of speech, freedom of mobility, freedom of religion or any of the other multiple meanings attached to the term *human rights* in this chapter. And the recent human rights violations that the Carter administration had singled out for criticism did not arise *because* of the dictatorial nature of the government but because of the unjust application of dictatorial control.

This explanation of the lack of correlation, however, loses much of its appeal when one examines the pattern of correlations of these items with other related questions. For example, both items are related to the importance of speaking out when other countries violate the human rights of their citizens and at about the same level: r=.22 with the importance of stopping dictatorships and r=.30 with support for the principle of criticizing human rights violations. Moreover, all three questions correlate significantly with the item about refusing trade with countries that violate human rights.

Even with good empirical as well as linguistic logic, then, two similar terms—*dictatorship* and *human rights violation*—may not touch the same nerve in the public. The temptation to read inferences from public thinking on a single item can be seen to be a most risky enterprise. Although the use of multiple items does reduce the risk, this example illustrates that the problem can still arise even when there are multiple items.

Bibliography

Bibliography*

Bardes, Barbara and Oldendick, Robert. "Beyond Internationalism: A Case for Multiple Dimensions in the Structure of Foreign Policy Attitudes." *Social Science Quarterly* 59 (1978):496-507.

Bishop, George; Oldendick, Robert; and Tuchfarber, Alfred. "Effects of Question Wording and Format in Political Attitude Consistency." *Public Opinion Quarterly* 42(1978): 81-92.

Bishop, George; Oldendick, Robert; and Tuchfarber, Alfred. "Experiments in Filtering Political Opinions." *Political Behavior* 2(1980):339-369.

Bishop, George; Oldendick, Robert; Tuchfarber, Alfred; and Bennett, Stephen. "Effects of Opinion Filtering and Opinion Floating: Evidence from a Secondary Analysis." *Political Methodology* 6(1979):293-309.

Bishop, George; Oldendick, Robert; Tuchfarber, Alfred; and Bennett, Stephen. "Pseudo-Opinions on Public Affairs." *Public Opinion Quarterly* 44(1980):198-209.

Cohen, Bernard C. *The Public's Impact on Foreign Policy.* Boston: Little, Brown and Company, 1969.

Converse, Philip E. and Schuman, Howard. "'Silent Majorities' and the Vietnam War." *Scientific American* 5(1970):17-25.

---

*Works given full bibliographic information in the notes have not been included.

Etzioni, Amitai. "MINERVA: A Study in Participatory Technology." Working Paper I. New York: Center for Policy Research, Inc., 1972.

Fischer, Elizabeth. "Change in Anomie in Detroit from the 1950s to 1971." Ph.D. dissertation, University of Michigan, 1973.

Hargrove, Irwin. *Presidential Leadership*. New York: MacMillan, 1966.

Hoffman, Ross and Levack, Paul, eds. *Burke's Politics: Selected Writings and Speeches on Reform, Revolution and War*. New York: Alfred A. Knopf, 1949.

Kettering Foundation. *Hard Choices: The American Public and U.S. Foreign Policy*. Dayton: Charles F. Kettering Foundation, 1978.

Lane, Robert E. and Sears, David. *Public Opinion*. Englewood Cliffs, NJ: Prentice-Hall, 1964.

Lenski, Gerhardt and Leggett, John. "Caste, Class and Deference in the Research Interview." *American Journal of Sociology* 65 (1960):463-467.

Marascuilo, Leonard and Amster, Harriet. "Survey of 1961-1962 Congressional Polls." *Public Opinion Quarterly* 28 (1964): 497-506.

Mueller, John E. *War, Presidents, and Public Opinion*. New York: John Wiley and Sons, 1973.

Robinson, John P. *Public Information about World Affairs*. Ann Arbor: Survey Research Center, University of Michigan, 1966.

Robinson, John P. and Holm, John D. *The Public Looks at Foreign Policy: A Report from Five Cities*. Cleveland: Communication Research Center, Cleveland State University, 1977.

Rugg, Donald. "Experiments in Question Wording II." *Public Opinion Quarterly* 5 (1941):91-92.

Schuman, Howard. "Two Sources of Anti-War Sentiment in

America." *American Journal of Sociology* 78 (1973):513-536.

Turner, Charles and Martin, Elizabeth, eds. *Surveys of Subjective Phenomena: Summary Report.* Washington: National Academy Press, 1981.

Turner, Charles and Krauss, Elissa. "Fallible Indicators of the Subjective State of the Nation." *American Psychologist* 37 (1978):456-470.

Verba, Sidney; Brody, Richard; Parker, Edwin; Nie, Norman; Polsby, Nelson; Ekman, Paul; and Black, Gordon. "Public Opinion and the War in Vietnam." *American Political Science Review* 61 (1967):317-333.

Index

DR. JOHN P. ROBINSON is a professor of sociology at the University of Maryland and the director of its Survey Research Center. While at the Institute for Social Research at the University of Michigan and the Communication Research Center at Cleveland State University, he directed and reported on many national and local surveys. Professional journals have featured his works on survey methodology, public opinion formation and change, and the impact of the mass media on public opinion. He is the author of *How Americans Use Time* and the senior author of *Measures of Political Attitudes* and *Measures of Social Psychological Attitudes.*

DR. ROBERT MEADOW is a professor in the Department of Political Science at the University of California at San Diego and a member of the Communication Program on that campus. Before moving to California, he was the director of the Survey Research Center at the University of Kentucky. He is the author of *Politics as Communication,* a coeditor of *Presidential Debates: Media, Electoral and Policy Perspectives,* and a frequent contributor to political science and communication journals, including *Communication Research* and *American Politics Quarterly.* He is currently working as a political consultant to Tom Shepard & Associates in San Diego.